BIRTHING

(A woman's story and guide to the successful delivery of a brilliant idea!)

April Jeffries

Visit the authors website:

www.ideabirthing.com

DEDICATION

For Lonnie, my brother, my friend, my fan.

ACKNOWLEDGMENTS

First, last and always I want to acknowledge and thank the ever-loving Source of all wisdom, truth and brilliant ideas.

Second, I want to thank my girlfriends who have pushed, helped, encouraged, and motivated with patience and kindness when there were plenty of other things they could have been doing. They include Gisele Simmons, Brenda Conner-Bey, CB Bowman, Doreen Stephens and Wendy Hill.

Third, I am overwhelmed with love and appreciation for my family. My mom Gee Gee (who is too nervous to read my writing), my sisterly advocate Ginger, my awesome daughters Jacci and Shannon and my keeper-of-a-husband Michael; all of whom have held my hand in one way or another through the stages of my personal idea birthing.

CONTENTS

Fertility

There are times in our lives when we are particularly open to receiving the seed of an idea that will lead us down the path of intense creativity. Sometimes abundant love will expand us to newer ground. More often, unhappiness will force the exposure of a new concept, providing the turning point where the pain of standing still is greater than the fear of doing something completely different. The atmosphere is swollen with possibilities, generating enough energy to create a change from the way things were, toward the way things are going to be. As our story begins, you will see how "discontent" is often nothing more than divine fertile ground providing the ideal environment for bringing something into this world that wasn't there before.

****

"Under normal conditions there is an extremely effective barrier that is thick and impenetrable and prevents anything from entering into the majestic womb. However, during the fertile period, the situation changes dramatically and the chemical change within this potent environment is really quite remarkable. The barrier becomes very clear, with a much thinner consistency, and actually helps rather than hinders the migration of a chosen sperm on its quest towards impregnating the patiently waiting egg."
The Pregnancy Countdown

CHAPTER 1

Psssst! Don't you remember? We thought about this a while ago.

For me, it usually happens in a whisper; a hushed, fleeting thought that slips secretly into the most efficient, goal-oriented conversation. It literally startles me with its contrast of whimsical lightness against the hard, focused reality of a business meeting, a boss' tirade, or a performance review. And while I try to whisk it away like a bothersome gnat, it exhibits the unexpected cunning and determination of an intelligent being. The hushed thought waits. It hovers. It lingers; sometimes for seconds, sometimes for months, but it always returns with that little hint of cynicism.

See! I told you. We could have done that better.

Ideas. Floating, exchanging, shifting, mingling. I'm convinced they are alive.

I'm awakened from my reverie by my boss' voice, puffed in arrogance, but secretly carrying the anxiety of knowing that he is asking the impossible. "Okay, so we need to replace this plan with a new one. Spending down by 25%, sales up by 35%--that's the formula. Any questions?

"How are we supposed to do *that*?" Poor Jane. She was relatively new.

"Just listen and do what I tell you to do!" he says sharply. "First of all, we're going to introduce our new and exciting innovation six months earlier than planned. Yes, that will give us more revenue this year instead of waiting until next. That ought to get us halfway there." We sat in familiar amazement watching him convince himself that he had just come up with a good idea. That project was already over budget and far behind the original timetable. Can you say Titanic? "Beyond that, we'll need to get creative. Think outside the box, people; raise prices perhaps, cut some spending. And make sure those numbers get us back to plan."

Our company makes ordinary consumer products. You know, toothpaste, soap, toilet paper, that kind of stuff. The good news is that people will always need the things we sell. The bad news is, "New!" and "Exciting!" are words that are rarely used.

Usually everything runs fairly steady around here. Every so often a new technology, such as motorized toothbrushes or steam released aromatherapy in our soaps, will find its way into our categories, changing those sales charts from flat lines to glorious spikes. Managers become heroes and win awards at the Christmas party. But that rarely happens. When sales slow down and we start to fall short, suddenly they expect toilet paper to change the world.

It took months for me to get Brian's buy-in of this new product he so casually referred to. My boss, Brian Cabu, came into the company at a middle management level and was clearly promised a future "seat at the table." He knew he needed an immediate "win" to secure the conditional carrot. I remember using that to my advantage to finally convince him that what I was proposing was a big idea. It took advantage of the whitening technology that brought over-the-counter dental hygiene to a new level. But once again, there were limits to how far you could push whiter teeth.

"So, we move up the timetable on the new product and cut spending. You guys always pad these budgets. I know you can figure out a way to do it. And get those sales people pushing extra inventory out there. Once it's on the shelf, somebody will buy it. If we have to, we'll take it back later, but we've got numbers to make."

He barks out these desperate orders as if they actually make sense. And we, his loyal team of experts, nod in agreement as if we believe we are being sent to play a game that is winnable.

But once we are out of the conference room, assumingly beyond the earshot of our intimidating leader, genuine feelings bubble to the surface like comic strip balloons.

"Yeah, right!" said with a sarcastic drawl.

"Didn't we have this conversation last month?"

"Is that legal?"

"I want what he's been smoking!"

My mind plays out an alternate scenario. In it, I go back and tell him that it's just not going to happen. Not like this. I actually have an inkling of a thought that maybe he would listen to me. Maybe I could convince him to let a few of us put our heads together to try and find reasonable ways to close the gap; ways that wouldn't risk the success of the only new news we'd had in years or compromise the integrity of the business.

After all, I'd been around for a while and had pulled many proverbial rabbits out of the hat to make commitments that should have never been made in the first place. In fact, while our relationship couldn't be described as "close friends," I believe that Brian has a healthy respect for me. Maybe we are at the point where I could honestly tell him that the better strategy now would be to start dialing down the expectations. Maybe not.

I was all too familiar with where this latest round of unreasonable requests was heading. Unrealistic objectives, month after month, required pages of explanations for breaking the latest promise. Quality standards are conveniently forgotten as we push through product that we really shouldn't be selling and that our customers really don't want. Strange people from the eleventh floor who only come down when something is terribly wrong, looking over your shoulder watching, waiting, offering you "help" that will require more explanation, i.e. work.

And the worst part was the way your business results got all tangled up in your personal self. You start to question your choices and decisions. Suddenly you're eating lunch by yourself, conversations stop when you enter the room, information comes to you from third removed sources. The organization has a way of equating a business that doesn't meet its numbers with a person that is clearly a *loser*. I've seen it happen. It is a fate worse than hell.

Remember me? It's not too late! C'mon, let's walk away from this craziness once and for all. Perfect timing. The little gnat was back.

"Shut up!" I hope I didn't say that out loud.

On my way home, I try to feel angry about the late nights looming ahead. Throwing out a plan that took months to create and replacing it in days always meant dinner at the office, conference rooms reeking of left over pizza, stale breath, and short tempers. But this time I can't even get angry. I don't know if that's good or bad. I just can't feel anything. I breathe deeply as I lock the car and walk up the driveway toward the front door. Along the walkway is a mini garden I planted months ago. I stop to see if anything has started blooming yet.

I love my little piece of suburbia. We purposely chose to live close to the city, but not in it. Somehow the energy of urban activity, while exciting, was often overwhelming. I remember arguing with Franklin about raising our kids in the city. I mean, I was a product of the concrete jungle and had no issue with above and below neighbors, or the rules of elevator navigation. But Franklin felt strongly that kids needed fresh air and open space. In the end, I gave in. In hindsight, this little oasis of stillness has kept me sane.

I never liked the streets of premade uniform houses, perfectly squared and measured to orderly and specific constraints. We eventually found this neighborhood where every house on the block was different and had its own unique personality as did the people living within them. Young families and old, dogs, cats, and pet bunnies and a myriad of cultures made this eclectic mix of characters and professions exactly what we were looking for.

I especially love this time of the year. We've planted all kinds of things that I don't know the name of, but looked pretty at the nursery. Nothing is blooming yet, but there are lots of buds, lots of brilliant, vibrant, three-dimensional promise. Somehow, in this special place I can hear myself think; at least before I open the door.

I gingerly hold my cell phone between my teeth while fumbling through my cute but not very practical purse, trying to discern the shape of my key ring among all the other crap I carry in that bag. In a convoluted way I know I'm stalling. This is the last remotely calm moment I will have to myself until I crawl into bed in what, five hours? Five hours is a long time.

I push the key into the lock and immediately hear Maybelline barking on the other side of the door. I remember when she was a puppy and we first saw her in the shelter. Her eyes had these thick black lines around them, and the girls thought she looked like she was wearing makeup. She was truly a beautiful Setter, but how come Maybelline didn't have that super doggie sense where she would actually bark *before* I put the key in the door? If I were lying on the floor having a heart attack, Maybelline would definitely not be the kind of dog to miraculously speed dial 911. Come to think of it, I would never survive a heart attack in my house. Never.

Suddenly, chaos on the other side of the door comes alive. Maybelline's nails scratch against the hard wood floor as she slides to greet me. The TV is blaring. Brandy is inside screaming at the top of her lungs, "Mommy home! Mommy home!" Dee, who is thirteen, is on the phone and clearly annoyed by the eruption of noise that has interrupted her conversation. "Brandy, shut up! I'm on the phone!" At eleven months, Brandy thinks shut up means scream louder and, by the way, is a hysterically funny thing to say. My husband Franklin, thinking he's helping, adds to the craziness, yelling back at the baby, "Brandy, please. Mommy will be here in a second!"

I push the door open with my foot, grab my briefcase, purse and several grocery bags and throw them inside.

"Hi, Babe." Franklin is at the computer focused on his latest article. Brandy is in her walker, half jumping, and half pushing herself toward me still screaming this time with absolute delight, "Mommy, Mommy!" I feel like Frederica Flintstone as Maybelline comes running at me with her big furry paws, knocking me off balance. I struggle to stay on my feet.

"Maybelline, no! Down, girl!" Didn't I teach her what "down girl" meant?

Dee holds out the phone. "Mom, it's for you. I was on the other line with Stephanie, so don't talk too long, okay?"

My sharp, critical look of disdain, which is intended to reclaim my powerful mother role, soars over her teenage head. This is going to be a long night.

"Hello?" I wedge the phone between my shoulder and neck as I pick Brandy up out of the walker.

"Hi, it's Brenda."

"Oh, hi, Brenda. What's up?"

"Are we still on for the movie on Saturday night? Remember, we promised to hold the date when we had dinner a few weeks ago."

As I pick her up, the baby starts pulling my glasses from my face. I pull them back amazed at the strength of her grip and stretch my focus to the calendar hanging heavily on the kitchen wall. It is a month behind. I try to keep the conversation going with small talk as I struggle to flip to the right page without losing my glasses to the wiggling baby in my arms. "So how's it going? What ever happened to that hunk you were going out with the last time we talked?"

"Who, Lenny? God, that was a month ago. He turned out to be a real jerk. Had to move on, you know."

"Oh, here it is, Saturday. Bren, I'm sorry, I can't do it. Franklin's out of town doing an interview for a follow up to that article he wrote in *Forbes*. Remember? The one about the new cell phone technology and the latest scandal."

"Actually, I *don't* remember." I'm shocked that she is actually annoyed. I didn't think it mattered that much. "You know, this isn't working out for me. It's like we've been trying to get together for months now and you always have something else to do."

"I know. It's been rough. My company isn't doing that great, and my boss is trying to prove some kind of point. Franklin's here with the kids most days, so when he has to travel, it's all on me."

"Can't you get a sitter?" I actually consider this for a second.

"I could, but I haven't been home too much lately. I feel like I owe it to the girls to spend some time with them, you know."

"Well, what exactly do you owe your friends? I mean, if you were a guy, I'd have dumped you a long time ago. You always feel guilty when it comes to Franklin and the girls, but your friends are the first to go. When you do that, it makes me feel like our relationship just doesn't mean anything to you."

I hate that "it makes me feel" therapy talk. "Brenda, really, I just walked in the door. I don't need this right now."

"Well, guess what, neither do I. It shouldn't be this hard just to see a movie, for God's sake. This is just taking too much energy for me. I have to go."

The phone slams on the other end. Dammit! She did *not* hang up on me! I click the receiver, trying to get a dial tone and start pushing hard on the buttons to redial her number.

I know exactly what I want to say. "I don't believe you! Do you have any idea what my life is like right now? I'm working twelve to fifteen hour days, my boss hates me, my husband is home all day and still considers everything he does "helping" me, I barely have time to pee, much less go to a movie with you.

I thought friends were supposed to understand, to be helpful. The last thing I need is someone else pulling at me right now. I mean, Jesus, how many grown people do I need to take care of in one lifetime? One week. One week I'd give you juggling my schedule and you'd be off to the therapist crying 'what about meee!' Maybe if you'd just get a life of your own, you wouldn't so easily judge the way I'm handling mine!"

I slam down the phone before I actually say any of that. No point in making this worse than it already is. Brandy giggles and points her chubby finger in my flushed face. "Mommy funny. Hee hee!"

I put Brandy down on the floor where she can safely crawl around and Franklin peeks his head in with one of those charming smiles of his. "Hey, lady. How was your day? Any thoughts on dinner?"

"Don't we have some chicken or something in there?" I barely hide my annoyance that there hasn't been any "thoughts" on dinner until now.

He sticks his head into the refrigerator "Chicken? You mean this right here?"

"Yes, Franklin. The yellowish-looking meat with the skin on it. Chicken."

"Okay, yeah, I can do this. I'll just cut it up, put some onions and green peppers on it, and throw it in the Wok. How's that?"

Did he totally miss my sarcasm or was he smart enough to just let it slide? "I have to get out of these clothes." My pumps and panty hose were suddenly so constricting, my breath starts to come in short erratic bursts.

"Okay, babe. You go put your feet up for a minute. I'll get this started."

"Where's Kelli?" Three daughters, each of them different, and I'm simply not complete until I've seen and talked to them all.

"Upstairs reading, I think."

I release my feet from the uncomfortable pumps and head toward the stairs. Green beans. I'd better tell him what to cook for a vegetable or else he won't think to do it. I turn to tell him and I see Brandy with her arms outstretched taking wobbly little steps in a futile effort to catch up to me. "Look! Franklin, she's walking!" Brandy had been so quick to speak, yet she showed little interest in walking. I had been quietly holding the thought in the back of my mind that if she didn't show some progress in the next couple of months I was going to take her to a specialist.

"Yeah, I wanted to surprise you. She took some steps earlier today and I cracked up laughing! Look at her wobble! Is that the funniest thing you've ever seen?"

"I can't believe you didn't call me! Oh my God! How cute is that?"

I hold out my arms. I want to meet her halfway but I resist the urge, knowing she needs to do this on her own. She makes her way across the kitchen floor with her brows furrowed, arms outstretched, eyes focused on the floor in front of her and the tip of her tongue peeking out through pursed lips--pure determination.

I anticipate her warmth against my body. I can smell the milk and afternoon's baby food on her breath and as she gets closer to me she starts to laugh with delight. In the space between her giggles I get pulled into an emptiness that catches me off guard. *First steps.* An incredible milestone. Too bad I wasn't there to see it. Once she successfully completes her journey I pick her up and hold her tight.

"Go see Daddy, sweet pea. Mommy will be back in a minute." I place her back down on her own two feet and, as she precariously toddles toward her father, I head upstairs overwhelmed with a feeling I don't completely understand.

As I enter my bedroom, the light on the alarm clock shows 8:30 PM. It's late. Dinner hasn't been started, my best friend hates me, the baby needs a bath, and I missed her first steps. I pull off the panty hose and feel the next level of release. I throw the navy blue dress on a pile of clothes intended for the cleaners and slip into my sweats and Gap tee shirt.

I peek into Kelli's room to see my middle child sitting on the bed reading a book. Kelli was four when she learned to read, and over the past two years she had become enamored with it. I'm happy that Kelli and I share a love of books. "Mommy, come sit. We need to talk," Kelli says and pats her hand patiently but firmly on the bed.

Oh no. I'm in trouble. The roles in this relationship had been reversed a long time ago and whenever Kelli said, "we need to talk" that meant, "Mom, you screwed up again." I see that she's reading *Matilda*. Damn. The Book Club.

"You know we were supposed to be at the reading club tonight, right, Mom?"

"Kelli, I'm so sorry. I got caught in a meeting, then I stayed to finish things up." As if a six-year-old really cares.

Kelli raises her hand in front of my face as if to say stop, please stop. "It's okay, Mom, really. It's just that, you know, if we're going to do this thing, we both have to do it. I like book club. I hate when we miss it. Remember, honor your commitments, Mom."

She was a master at repeating my lessons. No wonder people always said that Kelli had been here before. "You're right, baby girl. I'm sorry, and I'll try not to let that happen again."

She smiles up at me. "Want to read chapter four together? I started it already and it's really good. We can go back. I'll read one page, you read the next." I'm glad I'm so easily forgiven.

"Aren't you hungry?" I ask.

"Not really. Besides, Daddy's cooking. Dinner won't be ready until nine at best. Chicken, right?" She so totally gets it.

We both laugh. "Yeah, chicken." God bless her.

I cuddle up with my middle daughter and start to read. Kelli always laughs when I put on my acting voice to read out loud. At the bottom of the page I pass the book back to her and she picks up where I left off. Her reading is slightly broken, but her voice is soothing. *"Most children in Matilda's place would have burst into floods of tears. She didn't do this. She sat there very still and thoughtful. She seemed to know that neither crying nor sulking ever got anyone anywhere."*

As Kelli reads aloud, I drift into a light sleep, the kind where dreams are vivid and seem to go on for hours. I dream of giant white birds falling from the sky like snowflakes. I keep trying to pick them up and put them in a tiny wicker basket. Every time I put one in, Brandy waddles up to the basket, takes the bird back out, and throws it up into the sky, expecting it to fly again. But the birds hit the ground with a loud thump.

Dee starts screaming at me, "Mommy, just tell her. Tell her the birds are dead." I remember thinking if I tell her that, she'll cry, and I just can't handle that right now, so I keep picking up the birds and putting them in the basket. Then my boss comes pulling up into the driveway in a big black limousine and starts yelling at me that we're going to miss the plane. But, in my dream, I don't care. I pick up another dead bird and stuff it into the basket, trying desperately to salvage what I know cannot be saved.

I wake up curled in a fetal position on Kelli's tiny twin bed, still in my sweats and tee shirt. A pink flowered blanket is thrown over me and Kelli is snuggled up behind me with her arm thrown around my waist as if trying to keep me warm. I just lie there for a while listening to the steady rhythm of Kelli's breathing behind me, savoring the feeling of being wrapped in unconditional love.

I walk into the eight AM follow up meeting feeling kind of hopeful. On the way in I remembered this vendor whom I met with a few weeks ago who showed an interesting way to market some of our products. New video compressions allowed us to place ads in all kinds of online and mobile decision making situations. I figured if we couldn't make the products more exciting, maybe we could be innovative in how we talked to the women who bought them. Plus, it was cheaper than our normal television advertising and much more efficient. That way we could reduce some costs and still talk to our consumer base.

I sit next to Joe Martin, the new guy. I initially had thought that he would be working for me, but somehow he negotiated a direct reporting relationship to my boss. There is something about Joe that I just don't trust, but I figure I'll give him the benefit of the doubt until he proves differently. I notice Brian give Joe a pat on the back as he strides toward his designated seat at the head of the conference table.

"Joe informed me this morning that several of you were here late last night pulling together some contingency plans." Damn! They must have decided to stick around after I left yesterday. Joe starts passing out a thick presentation deck.

"Yes, Brian. We thought about what you said and figured out a way to pull about four months out of the timeline for our new product. That and a modest adjustment in price and we can get back to within pennies of the original plan."

I can't believe they're presenting this without my input. I'm going to put a nail in this before it gets out of hand. I flip through the presentation looking for something to pop out at me. I had pulled together a million of these presentations before. Hell, I was a master. And I knew, there was always a red flag. Always. The trick was to bury it when presenting, to find it when being presented to.

"Modest price increase? This looks pretty significant to me." There it is, the red flag, blaring like a foghorn. "Can you justify the price increase without any affect on how much we sell?" I glace over at Jane, who looks tired and ashen. She should know this. She's the one who developed the model that showed the relationship between pricing and cases sold and the findings were significant. Raise the price ten cents, sell a lot fewer cases. Jane looks down at her note pad, clearly embarrassed that she has been dragged into this.

"We don't think it'll make any difference. People love this brand. They'll pretty much pay what we ask," Joe responds. I'm really *not* liking this Joe guy.

"We've got a lot of studies, not to mention experience, that says different. I mean, at the very least we need to reach more people with the message. I spoke with this vendor yesterday who might have a marketing idea."

Brian interrupts my sentence. "Let's not make this any more complicated than it has to be. Joe seems to have thought this through. Let's just run with it." Brian would believe anything at this point. He starts spewing out directions to put this brilliant plan into action and never makes eye contact with me. I am officially invisible.

"Brian, let's at least run the model with the new price and get a worst case scenario." I hate the whiny sound of my voice right now. I pray that Jane speaks up. Silence.

"Let's roll, people. Follow Joe's lead on this one." Can't see me. Can't hear me.

And it's at that strategic moment of weakness, that fertile opening of clarity, the clever little thought pops back.

C'mon. We've seen this movie before and the ending really sucks.

Not now. Just give me minute to think clearly here.

Let's put that energy into making me *happen. We can do this!*

It is with that completely irrational thought that I throw all my normal groundedness and good sense to the wind. In that moment, I consider the chaotic turbulence of my life and realize how much I have given up following and carrying out someone else's plan, reasonable or not. Suddenly, it doesn't seem worth it. My fellow teammates walk ahead of me and I stop, surrounded by the cold barren stillness of padded cubicles. I hear the collective rumblings of my peers, my memory and my mind. And I make a choice.

We're gonna have soooo much fun.

I turn around and push open the door to the conference room that we had just exited. My boss, still gathering his papers and his weathered leather portfolio, looks up and is surprised to see me. "Was I not clear?" That little hint of annoyance in his question seals my internal deal.

"I quit." Did I say that?

DNA

Consider carefully what you bring to this process from a maternal position. Hear the words of those who know you best with a different ear and recognize what reverberates within. Make deliberate decisions about what you want to keep, what you want to change and what no longer suits you. When we tap into our unique DNA, we are drawn toward a life we were Destined to live. We Navigate the waters of our own experience and Adjust our antennae to tap into an inner compass. At this point in our story, watch the unfolding of the personal DNA she will bring as the birthing vessel of this new being.

****

"DNA is often compared to a set of blueprints, like a recipe or a code, since it contains the instructions needed to construct other components of developing cells. Therefore it is key to the determination of the physical, emotional, and intellectual qualities of the soon to be born infant."
The Miracle of Birth--Discovery Channel

CHAPTER 2

"Oh my God! Oh my God! Oh my God! What did I just do?" I throw the cardboard box on the back seat of my very expensive car, which, by the way, is nowhere near being paid for. All of my office belongings are contained in one torn moving box that I managed to confiscate from the packing floor: a picture of Franklin and the girls, my crystal "Make a Difference" award I won last year, my bankers desk lamp, and the contents of my upper left drawer (hose, clear nail polish, gum, earrings, lipstick, .7 pens that I like to write with, emergency credit card, make up bag, and HP calculator.)

I have trouble putting the key in the ignition. My hands are shaking. I pull up to the gate and reach for my ID that, when swiped across the all-knowing electric eye, magically allows those who belong to enter and leave the premises. But I have no ID. They collected that on my way out. I back up and redirect my car to the lane where visitors are sent, and Michael, the guard, picks up where the electric eye left off, confused as to whether or not I should be allowed to leave. Michael recognizes me. He is annoyed that I've forgotten my card and pushes the button waving me on. He doesn't realize I didn't forget my corporate identification; I gave it back.

"Okay, okay, okay. I'm not going to panic," but already I'm wishing I'd kept a brown paper bag in that upper left drawer. I pull out my cell phone and start to call Franklin, but quickly realize I am not ready to have this conversation with him. I need to be in control when I tell him and right now I need to throw up. Beth. My best friend since college. Always positive. Always supportive. Yeah, that's what I'll do. I'll call Beth.

"Oh my God! You had your Norma Rae moment and you didn't even warn me it was coming. Couldn't you have put me on speaker phone or something?" Beth says, clearly excited for me. How easy it is to be excited when someone else quits his or her job.

"It's not funny, Beth. I just lost my job. I have no income. I'm unemployed." I am starting to hyperventilate again.

"First of all, you didn't lose your job; you quit. There's a difference, I guess. The point is, you're free! Listen, don't panic. I'll call Jolie and Brenda and tell them to meet us at the Marquis after work."

"Not Brenda. She's not speaking to me again," I quickly respond, feeling like that stupid phone call happened years ago. I can't believe it was only last night.

"What happened? Never mind. Just Jolie then. But don't panic. We'll meet you there at six o'clock." I look at my watch. It is 1 PM. I park my car and spend the rest of the day wandering through the city, wondering what it is like to be homeless. I listen for a supporting thought from my internal voice. Nothing.

Beth hugs me as the young girl at the door leads us to Jolie, who is sitting at the bar, talking sternly to someone on her cell phone. Jolie acknowledges us with a nod and keeps on talking as she picks up her bag and falls in line behind us, never missing a beat.

"Hi, Candice." Beth calls the waitress by the name on her tag. "Can you please bring us a round of Mojitos? And make my friend's here extra strong. Oh yeah, and some of that delicious guacamole you guys make. It's awesome." The young girl eagerly goes off to fulfill Beth's request. At first my back goes up in defense. A Mojito was not my first choice of drink. Then I realize I am grateful to have someone else take control and order for me.

"So what's your plan? Where do you go from here?" Jolie is fully with us now.

"I honestly don't know. Right now I just need some time to breathe, to get my head on straight. Tell me I'm not the stupidest idiot you ever met." I recognize the underlying neediness in my request.

"Well, not the stupidest. But you do need a plan, Tonto," Jolie responds. She is a lawyer; straight, to the point, always one for a plan.

How about we get to know each other better before we start planning. The voice was back. I hadn't heard from it since I left the office.

Beth verbally supports where my head was trying to take me. "Please! You don't need a plan. You need some air and a strong drink. This is no small move you've made here. Take your time and savor this for a moment." There is a moment of silent transition before Beth continues. "What did Franklin say?"

"I haven't told him yet. I needed to talk to you guys first. He's going to kill me." I can see in my mind the expression Franklin is going to make; that squinted, fast blinking look he gives me when he can't believe what just came out of my mouth.

"He won't kill you. Franklin's a good guy." Beth always liked Franklin. After she divorced Bobby #1 she used Franklin as her model for what she wanted next. She found him in Bobby #2 (for a while it was hard keeping track of her Bobbies) who seemed to make her happy although they never got married. Having children would be the only reason for them to "tie the knot," and clearly they hadn't made that decision yet.

"Yeah, knowing Franklin, he'll just freak out a little at first, then he'll sulk for a couple of days, then he'll be fine," Jolie says. She, on the other hand, is a divorce lawyer and drives Franklin crazy with her descriptions, stories, and all-knowing wisdom of extremely dysfunctional couples.

"No, he's gonna kill me. I mean, he's the creative one. I'm supposed to be the one with sense. I can't even speak to him intelligently about what I'm going to do. This is so not us. Franklin and I can hardly be called spontaneous." My voice starts to get that panicky resonance.

"That's true. You guys were engaged for like ten years." Thanks for that little reminder, Miss Jolie Practical.

"Seven." So there.

"Seven, ten, whatever. The point is you two aren't exactly risk takers, you know."

"Franklin won't be surprised." Beth has an interesting perspective on life. "Hell, I'm not. The truth is you've always wanted to do your own thing. I'm surprised you lasted this long. Remember in college we'd always be coming up with some business idea that would get us rich. If I recall correctly, you were always the one to initiate those kinds of conversations.

Listen, listen, listen.

"Yeah. We were usually in an altered state of some kind when that happened in college," I snap back. I know, I'm supposed to listen, but let's get real here.

"Oh, yeah." Beth remembers. I shake my head, disappointed that she didn't have a better comeback than *Oh, yeah.*

Beth redeems herself with a new thought. "Look, you're probably one of the most intelligent and creative people I know. That job never took advantage of all of you.

I mean, they owned the left side of your brain, but do they even know how brilliant your right side is?" Thank you, Beth. That was nice. The right side, left side thing was pretty clever. "I say you use this as a 'reinventing yourself' opportunity."

I take a long sip of my Mojito, hoping, at some point, an answer will surface. "If I were thinking, I probably would have saved more. Maybe I wouldn't have been so impulsive."

"Trust me. You have everything you need right this moment to do whatever you need to do." I wish I could believe that, Bethy Bear.

Believe it.

Jolie has been noticeably quiet. I get the feeling she wants to be supportive, but honestly doesn't know how. "Well, what are you going to do sweetie?" Do. Plan. Act. Jolie's A-type personality is helpful sometimes. At this particular moment, however, it is annoying.

"I haven't the foggiest. I've always had so many ideas for what I could do. Now I'm drawing a blank."

Don't worry you'll know when you're ready. Really?

Jolie's cell phone rings again, but before she answers, she shrugs and puts the palm of her hand on my face. "What the hell! Honey, we've been busting our butts for the past fifteen years. We all could use a break. Take it while you can."

At this moment I am so grateful to have these two women as friends. Being with them was like going home. They know the real me. They remind of a place and time when I was a different person, when my dreams were so much bigger. They awaken another side of me that has been asleep for a long time. Slowly I am rejuvenated. I am in a movie about strong women and believe in my heart that we are kindred sisters. Any moment we might use our spoons as mini microphones and break out singing "Ain't No Mountain High Enough."

It takes several more Mojitos before I am ready to face my husband.

"Don't you think you could have talked to me first?" This is not going well. Franklin is trying hard not to be angry, but then he starts that squinty thing again.

"I barely talked to *me* first. This was like, so weird, Franklin. Like the words just came out of my mouth. It's so not like me, I know. I just don't know what happened."

"We have enough money to make it for a little while don't we?" My husband was always a step removed from our household finances. He trusted me completely and I always did what was best for all of us; until now.

"Yeah, I saved a little. I'll figure this out, baby. Just give me some time, okay?" I hug him and put my head on his shoulder in a desperate attempt to be helpless and in need of a hero.

He takes the bait and relinquishes a comforting arm around me. "You know what? It's probably time you took a little break anyway. Hey, the girls would love to have you home for a while and maybe that will free me up to finish some projects I've been working on. I'm kind of proud of you. You seriously walked in, just like that, and quit?"

"Uh-huh," a sheepish reply that makes us both crack up laughing. I knew if I could just get him laughing, I could hold him off with the questions. It reminded me of when I broke the news that I was pregnant with Dee. We hadn't planned on having kids so soon. I remember the internal fluttering in my stomach and how I couldn't figure out if it was disappointment, excitement, fear, or a mixture of all three. I exhale. I'm tired.

"We'll be okay" he reassures me, just like he did fourteen years ago. I am certain he will buy a lotto ticket tomorrow.

****

It's been a rough night. At 3:00 in the morning I finally give in. There is no point in lying there staring at the ceiling. I take a long hot shower and make a delicious pot of tea. With a hint of ginger, crushed mint and pure cane sugar, I believe this is the best cup of tea I ever tasted. I absorb the rich delicious creaminess with all of my senses and, for a moment, I relish the feeling of unlimited possibilities.

Savor the moment.

Yes, savor the moment. Didn't we talk about savoring earlier? I need to relearn how to do that. I push on the door to return the canister of sugar to the carousel and all kinds of mismatched Tupperware, metal bowls, and unused pitchers, block its smooth opening. I force it and several canisters and bowls fall out on the floor at my feet, making a loud ruckus. Maybelline, who has followed me into the kitchen hoping to share a midnight snack, looks up at me as if to say *shhhh*. My family sleeps on.

One by one I start sorting. The things I use all the time get a special place for easy accessibility. The things I like, but don't have tops that fit, have to go. The things I never really use, have to go. The things that came from unknown sources, have to go. After making these brutal but clear decisions, there is a lot of empty space in my kitchen carousel. This time I will carefully decide what to fill it with. I move on to the pots and pans and closets and the junk drawers and, in the act of performing these rote activities, I sort things out in my mind.

I'm amazed that my husband didn't react more dramatically. He had every right to be angry. I mean, you don't just up and quit your job like that without at least discussing it with the people who will have to support you through your madness. I'm not sure I would have handled it so well if he had done the same.

I bought some time last night, giving him the opportunity to be the hero for a while, but I was going to have to get moving on something soon. I know I want to go out on my own, but what does that mean exactly? Doing what? I have had so many interests and likes and hobbies, I should be able to combine them with my business skills and do something cool.

But the truth is, having too many is almost as bad as not having any at all. I have so many ideas in a given day sometimes it's hard to catch one. They slide in and out of my grasp like a slippery fish, drifting around in flimsy seductive patterns that shift with the tides. And the moment

I look at one too hard it disappears, eluding me like a word that dances on the tip of my tongue and never quite makes it out of my mouth. I keep trying to force this feeling into something specific, something definite that I can work on, plan against, program into my Blackberry.

Let it come to you.

What? Oh man, this is so *not* me. Don't you understand? Things don't come to me. I make things happen. That's the way it has always worked for me.

Really?

What was that supposed to mean? As I toss another unmatched saucepan into the had-to-go pile, I consider that maybe it wasn't me after all. The progress that I had made in the past, all the accomplishments, all the successes, they all had a certain element of serendipity to them. The right person shows up at the right time. The right opportunity surfaces in the right place. The right conversation reveals an unexpected right connection.

I went after things, yes, but could I really take all the credit for it? And as I enter this uncertain new phase of my life, I realize that the answer is out there but right now I haven't a clue. And that is a scary thought. That takes it completely out of my control. And I wonder if I ever had control to begin with.

At best, all I can do at this point is set an intention. An intention to create a life that is truly an extension of who I am, that allows me to give of myself and my talents fully, to live by my own lights, to be able to spend time with my family, to give something good to the world; and, oh yeah, make a lot of money in the process. That's not too much to ask for. Is it?

The Perfect Mate

The perfect mate is essentially, a hole to be filled, a gap to be bridged, a problem to be solved. The world is filled with so many situations that require a solution, as you'll see as our story continues. The challenge is to find one that leverages your specific gifts. The problem, and what you bring to solve it, will provide the benefit and reason why your new idea makes perfect sense. Whatever we create, we must envision, on some level, how it will touch the world. Therein lies the potential for brilliance.

****

"Females tend to select mates who have superior good sperm genes because it means that their offspring will not only be more viable, but they will inherit the genes and pass them on to future generations."
Science Magazine, Good Sperm

CHAPTER 3

I get out of bed and get my daughters ready for school, trying to keep to the normal routine as much as possible. For the most part, I am able to maintain the charade, but Kelli almost blows it with her first grade sensitivity.

"You're wearing jeans and sneakers to work today, Mommy?"

"Actually, I'm working at home today, pumpkin."

"Why? I like your office in the city." I knew I would someday regret the field trip we all took to "Mommy's office" when we had gone to see a Broadway matinee and I stopped in quickly to pick up a report I had forgotten. Kelli, in particular, loved being in the city. The fact that I had a

43

view overlooking all the midtown activity made it all the better. I remember how she pulled the rolling leather chair to the window and sat in silence, hypnotized by the crazy, chaotic downtown energy.

"Well, I'll be home today." It's not like I wasn't going to tell the girls that I had quit my job. I just wasn't ready yet. Thankfully the school bus came just in time to keep me from having to give an answer to the why question. As Dee, my beautiful, logical, in-her-own-world teenage daughter, starts to board the bus, she turns as if she has forgotten something.

"I'm glad you're home, Mom," she says. I didn't even think she'd been listening. "Hey, can you pick me up some graph paper? I need it for my Math project." For a moment, I panic. If I'm not careful, I'll quickly become the errand delivery girl. Then I realize I've always been the errand delivery girl; only now I don't have to fit it between meetings and lunches. The accordion door of the school bus slams behind her, just like any other day.

Now it's just the baby and me. I decide to give Franklin the morning off just to keep on his good side. Kelli has a seven-year-old birthday party to go to on Saturday and I'm thinking it would be nice to have a card already purchased two whole days in advance, as opposed to our normal frantic routine of stopping at the CVS on the way to the party. I sit down to feed Brandy and turn on the television. Daytime television is scary.

I flip through the courtroom cases and talk shows. Oh my God, people putting their business out on the street, "baby daddy" drama, cross dressers, divorce court. Damn! So many people with issues, no sense of focus, wandering through life like this is normal behavior. First, I think they must be actors. Then I realize, you can't make this stuff up.

I change the channel. I vow that if I ever see any of my daughters on Jerry Springer I will beat them senseless. I change the channel. Dr. Phil has women who continue to stay in abusive marriages. It is painful watching the strange behavior that fills the void of self-esteem. I change the channel. Ellen has a woman doctor who gave up her practice to design and sell shoes. She made millions selling the cutest little shoes that don't hurt your feet! Brilliant. I change the channel.

Four women are discussing the news events of the day. The president of an Ivy League university is under fire because he publicly commented that women are inherently dumber than men and that's why there aren't many in math and science. It reminded me of the number of times I had to prove to Brian that my numbers made sense. How annoying. Why in the world would a college president go on a show with four strong women anchors after making a statement like that? They ream him. What an idiot.

So many problems, so little time.

I get Brandy and myself dressed, remembering what a feat it was to do this after she was born. I was with her on maternity leave for three months. At least she used to sit still. These days I had to wrestle her down. She is amused at my attempts to control her. I just crack her up.

Since children's birthday parties always catch me off guard, I usually keep a stack of gift certificates to Barnes and Noble in my desk drawer. But this time, what the heck. Let's go for a real present from a real toy store this time. A casual stroll through Toys R Us was something I had never done. There was always a purpose, a reason, a time crunch, that had me more focused on the next thing I had to do instead of the task at hand. But on this day, we take our time.

It's amazing the things we see. Oh, to be a kid again. There are so many things I want for myself; a science kit that actually makes crystals out of nothing, interactive games that monitor hand movements and adjust the level of play accordingly. And the dolls. Barbie has become the role model for any young girl's dream: doctor, lawyer, professional skater, or simply beautiful.

Then there are the newest versions of my little girl fantasies; bad girls who have the nerve to wear colorful clothes, carry guitars, and ride motorcycles while heading to jobs as teachers, scientists, and brain surgeons. It makes me remember what it's like to dream. I turn down the aisle and literally bump into Emily Watson. We had met at a kid's party several weeks ago, and she, too, had her one-year-old in tow.

"Emily, how are you? I've actually been meaning to call you. How's your business going?" I remembered that Emily had told me she was a stay-at-home Mom. But she had an interesting hobby. Emily created these wonderful lotions, creams, and facial products in her kitchen during her "spare time" and had dreamed of someday opening a retail store. She had given me a hand lotion sample that smelled like lavender and lime and immediately made me feel like I'd been to the spa.

"Business? Oh, you mean the aroma products. I haven't done too much lately. Jeff has been working hard and hasn't been home much, so I haven't had too much time to focus. Plus, he's in marketing, you know. He seemed to think it was a small idea."

"Well, all I know is, by the time I finished talking to you, I was ready to buy a case of the stuff." I wondered what kind of analysis Jeff had done to determine the size of this "small" business.

"Really? I don't know, it was just taking up an awful lot of time, you know. Hey, I wouldn't expect to see you out and about this time of day. Are you on vacation?"

"Yeah. Taking a mental health day." Still not ready to share my big move with everybody. "But about your products; you really should expose them to more people. Moms like us who can appreciate how they make us feel. I just remembered feeling pampered at a time when I would normally feel frazzled. You solved a problem for me that day. It was quite an experience. One that I would pay to have again."

You just gave her a wonderful gift. She had no idea of the benefit she was providing.

"Really? I guess I never thought about it that way," Emily says, clearly uncomfortable with praise and compliments.

"I think you have something there," I respond, refusing to let the moment pass.

"Well, I have to go. Maybe I'll see you at Marcia's party next week."

I thought it best to let it go, but I just couldn't. "By the way, if you have time, I'd love a couple of jars of that lavender body cream. Just let me know how much it costs." I see her face light up just a little.

"Sure. I also have a great exfoliation cream for your face. The secret ingredient is cane sugar. It's amazing."

"Great. I'll take some of that, too. Just don't give away those secrets to everybody. Somebody may take it and run with it."

"Yes. You're right." We laugh, we hug, and I leave, wondering if she will really bring the product the next time we meet. I silently wonder how many dreams get aborted before they even have a chance to develop.

I end up at Barnes and Noble anyway. While I bought one of those adorable colorful dolls at Toys R Us, I'm feeling like I want to anchor the gift with something a little more educational. As I walk into the store, there is a display of a new author. At first, I walk by it completely. But there is something about it that calls me back. It is a children's book, but I get the feeling adults will enjoy it, too; a cross between fantasy and science fiction. The display is not overwhelming, but is beautiful and magical in its own way. I buy one, thinking it is something that Kelli and I might enjoy reading together someday.

I open to the back cover and see the picture of the author. She actually looks a lot like Emily. I wonder if anyone had ever told this budding young author that her idea was small and how she dealt with that. I wonder if Emily would ever have a big colorful display of her aroma products drawing some unsuspecting consumer to it and making her buy it when she had come into the store for something totally different. I wonder what this author's secret is and, if I can figure it out, I'll tell Emily to add it as an ingredient in her face cream.

Think of the problem she solved. Kids are reading again.

By the time Brandy and I get back, the girls are home from school, Franklin is at his computer working, and I decide to cook a special dinner. It had been a long time since we all sat and ate together before eight o'clock. We talk about our days. We even laugh. A lot. It is very, very nice.

Conception

The fusion of your DNA and the seed of a greater need will occur within the perfect environment that you've been preparing since this journey started. We never see the actual act of conception but imagine that it requires the breaking down of energy, chemicals, and substances; a gelatinous mess from which a particle of clarity begins to form. As our story continues, you will witness the environment, the examples and the moment that the conception of her brilliant idea takes place.

****

"When the two nuclei fuse, their genetic material combines together to create a zygote, which is what a fertilized egg cell is called. What goes on invisibly remains deeply mysterious. The genetic information dissolves into an amorphous soup-like state, only to reconstitute into the structure of a human being. Every cell knows what it is programmed for."
Scientific American, Conception Explained

CHAPTER 4

There are so many things I could do, things I've been meaning to do for years: clean the garage, wash the windows, do some laundry. There is a strange sense of freedom; choices that I never had the option to make before. Somehow the morning slips by and I wonder if I'm capable of handling all of this autonomy.

The afternoon is committed. Brenda is finally talking to me again and, once I told her about the job thing, she calmed down considerably. She decided that now that I had all the time in the world, it was her job to make sure I stayed connected. Brenda runs our local children's museum. She is the consummate organizer and was always joining some non-profit board or organization.

As annoying as Brenda could be sometimes, I have to admit she has a good heart. Her latest interest was this venture that helped young girls develop confidence and skills for the business world. She is going out of town and asked me to attend in her place to check it out. I still feel a little bad about not going to the movies with her that night, so I agree to go to this one meeting for her. But I make no promises to join. I figure, I do need to take advantage of networking opportunities.

The meeting is being held at the house of the organization's founder, which is located in one of the richest areas of our town. Sprawling lawns and circular driveways rise with elegance as I count by twos for the address I need to find. I end up parking up the street since so many people have already arrived. I'm not that late, but apparently everyone else is right on time. The crunching gravel beneath my feet underscores the chatter coming from the back of the house. I enter around the side and see a huge white tent protecting at least a hundred crisply dressed women from the intense rays of the sun. Somehow I hadn't expected it to be this big.

I pick up Brenda's nametag from the table, one of the last to be claimed, and scope out the set-up, looking to see if there is anyone here that I know. A caterer wearing black pants with a white-collar shirt comes up to me carrying a tray of cute little cucumber sandwiches and slightly grilled tuna. He is a young guy, maybe in his twenties, and I get the sense that he is inwardly laughing at the pretentiousness of it all.

"You guys got any real food in the back?" I ask him as I hungrily pierce an unsuspecting cucumber sandwich.

He looks at me almost unbelievingly, not sure how to take me. "Ribs and chicken at the caterer's after party. You want to come?" He decides to take the risk.

"Well, obviously I'm going to still be hungry after this. Let's just hope it doesn't go on for too long."

"No, seriously," he says, "you can come. I'll tell them you're with me." How cute. He is flirting.

"Honey, trust me, I'm old enough to be your mother. Well, maybe your young aunt." This is weird. I honestly gave up flirting a long time ago. Too much energy. "Plus, I'm very, very married."

"Like, two kids and a house in the suburbs married?"

"Three kids. And a dog." I'm almost embarrassed by the extreme category that describes my life.

He shrugs as if that is perfectly acceptable. "Hey, that's cool. You know, desperate housewives are hot!" and he winks at me. "Only half kidding."

"Excuse me, Monty." A heavy woman dressed in white and emanating with importance interrupts our conversation. This must be either the owner of the house or some critical organizer type person. "I hate to interrupt your conversation with," she focuses on my incorrect nametag and gives me a cordial nod, "Brenda here, but we seem to be out of those shrimp dumplings at the buffet and I paid for those scallop and bacon horsd'oeuvres. I haven't seen them yet." I start to tell her my name isn't Brenda, but I could tell she didn't care.

"Mrs. Eldridge, I know how you like to do things. I'm pacing this so that you have a constant stream of deliciousness right up until the very end. This place looks so beautiful, I don't think people are going to want to leave." Monty is a charmer, I see.

"Ooohhh!" She falls for it. "Well, don't wait too long. Those are my favorites."

"They'll be out in the next serving," he says as she heads toward a group of prospects.

I'm impressed with the way he handled her, but don't want him to get in any trouble. "I better let you get back to work before your boss starts getting complaints from the client."

"My boss? That would be *me*." His chest puffs proudly.

Pay attention.

"Therefore, I can fraternize with anyone I want. Not to mention, Mrs. Eldridge wouldn't dare complain. My food is too good. I've seen her do a few of these events. She's actually pretty amazing. First level kick off, we invite everybody. Medium quality horsd'oeuvres and cash bar. Always a cash bar."

"I guess she doesn't want a bunch of rich drunks knocking over the fine china." We both laugh, grateful that I was able to capture what he was obviously thinking, but wouldn't dare say.

"Exactly. Next go round will be for special guests with specific and targeted resources. Food is better. Wine flows freely. Once she goes in for the final commitment, it's typically a smaller group, interest confirmed, very dedicated. We're talking full dinner; lobster, filet mignon, chilled wine by the bottle and open bar. It works every time."

"I guess we could all learn a few things from her," I say, also impressed with the fine-tuned strategy.

"I already have. She knows what she's doing. She's launched a few of these non-profits, and they always run like clockwork and attract sizeable chunks of money. But at this point, if you want anything stronger than my fine sizzle punch, you have to cough up some cash at the bar. Or come to the after party." He slips that one in again, but I ignore him.

"Your own catering thing, huh?"

"Yep. Dropped out of law school to follow a dream. Haven't looked back since."

"Congratulations, Monty. That must have taken a lot of guts."

"Definitely worth the risk."

Another woman with a coded nametag begins to shepherd the mingling guests toward a large media room. "I think your meeting is about to start. I was serious about the after party. My personal guest?" Persistent does not begin to describe this guy.

"Thanks anyway, Monty. Good luck." I smile at him and walk away. As I turn, I practically tumble over a little girl, maybe five or six years old, no taller than my thigh. She is standing with a handful of change and balled up dollar bills in one hand and a can of Diet Coke in the other. She looks confused.

"Oh, my goodness, honey, be careful! Are you okay?"

"My Mom told me to get her a Diet Coke and she gave me a five dollar bill. Is this the right change?" She holds out her hand with the crumpled money in it. I stoop down so that I can be at her level and help her straighten out the money.

"Well, first thing is, you have to take good care of your money or else it won't take care of you. That's what my Mom always told me and it works for me."

She looks up at me with innocent eyes and smiles. "You're funny. The man said the soda cost one dollar and fifty cents."

"So let's count it." I take her over to a corner where we sit, criss cross applesauce, on the floor, and I show her my tricks for getting to the right change. She soaks it up like a sponge.

"Here's the other thing about money. If you hold on to it too tight, it never has a chance to breathe and grow. So you have to be generous. When you got the soda, there was a little glass with change in it. Did you see that?"

"I saw a glass with a little sign on it, but there was no change. It was empty."

"I want you to go back and take this quarter and put it in the glass. And as you do it, put a little thought in your head that says *let this quarter be of help to someone who could use it* and that's what will happen."

"How do you know?"

"Well, you don't. But you can imagine all the good things that might happen to that quarter now that you've made your wish on it. When you give the change back to your Mom, tell her that the Coke was a dollar fifty and you left an 18% tip for Monty. Then just walk away. Trust me, she'll be very impressed."

Nice.

The child smiles, grabs her change, starts to run away, then deliberately comes back and says, "Thanks, lady! My Mom never explained it to me like that. You should be a teacher or something." I watch her run back to the beverage set-up, hold up her quarter, and close her eyes, wishing on the monetary star. Then she drops the quarter in the glass marked tip and it clangs around until it settles on the bottom.

The meeting begins and everyone stands individually to introduce themselves. I have a difficult moment, surrounded by all this affluence, wondering if quitting was a smart thing to do. I mean, if nothing else, the job did pay well. It is almost my turn to speak. I am not sure how to introduce myself behind the vice presidents and CEO wives. They all go into long descriptions of the impressive groups they belonged to and the important things they had done in their lives. I excuse myself and go to the bathroom before they get to me. I spend the rest of the evening standing in the back, listening inconspicuously.

I cannot hear the speaker's message. Every time I try to focus, the thoughts start slipping in again, this time in different but familiar voices:

You're the most brilliant, creative person I know.

Thanks lady. You should be a teacher or something.

Desperate housewives are hot.

I get that fluttery feeling inside and, in an unexpected moment of clarity, I know what I want to do.

Embryonic Development

No obvious physical changes are apparent to the outside world, but inside all kinds of miraculous things are happening. The nebulous form is starting to take shape within. Your infant idea is in a fragile form. Share sparingly, only with those who will be supportive and whose response will contribute positively to its growth. In our story, follow the process as the budding idea develops. Notice how questions and obstacles surface, but she puts them aside for later. Now is time to give your idea the space to form unhindered.

"The fertilized egg attaches itself within you, drawing nutrients and sustenance from you in its protected environment. An embryo forms quickly soon to develop its own tiny beating heart. As its evolution continues, it learns to respond to stimuli including pain, light and sound. The lungs, however, take a very long time to mature. The baby cannot breathe on its own."

Nova, The First Trimester

CHAPTER 5

I literally have the seed of an idea, a stake in the ground, something to get moving on. But it isn't exactly a vision. I always imagine a vision being clear and defined. I believe visionaries see and know exactly what they want, drawing a mental image of their dream that reality must catch up with. But what I have is not very clear. It is smoky and unformed. If I look at it too hard, it disappears. So I let it play alone and peek in occasionally to see how it is doing.

I am excited about the feeling I have, even though I know I can't exactly describe it. It's just a feeling; a beautiful, wonderful feeling of doing something good, something greater than myself; a feeling that this is what I was put here to do. Although this is bigger than I had expected and I don't have all the answers, intuitively I feel that I can do this and that I have everything I need to make it happen.

I start to tell Franklin about it, but somehow I know it's too early. As strongly as I feel on the inside, I'm just not in a place to defend it yet. It is too fragile, too delicate. I can't bear having someone question me about it or challenge me on it or even add something to it yet, risking its integrity, trying to force it in a direction that it isn't meant to go. I don't want it to fall into that category of old ideas that got talked about, laughed about, even bragged about, but never came to be. I can't bear that. This one is too important.

I decide to spend the day in silence, holding this idea close to me, spending time getting to know it better. Bonding with it, nourishing it, connecting with it so that when it is delivered, we both will be so much more than either of us on our own.

It's amazing what silence does. I'm not talking about the "holding back" kind of silence, when I'm angry or frustrated or I know that if something comes out of my mouth it will be the wrong thing. I'm talking about the kind of silence where I simply pay attention. I speak when I have to, but only when I have to. The rest of the time I just listen.

And it's quite amazing. Every book or magazine I pick up has a message for me. Kelli is watching TV and Sponge Bob confirms a thought I have been playing around with. It's so startling I do a double take. The more I stay open, the more the information just keeps flowing in, from all kinds of unexpected sources. It becomes a challenge to keep up with the messages and make wise choices as to what to include and what to let go of.

Sometimes when I'm not sure, I just wait. Whatever wants to be heard keeps coming back over and over again. It is a beautiful thing. The nebulous form in the distance is starting to take shape.

I lie here in darkness and complete silence, eyes wide open, Franklin snoring soundly beside me, my emotional rollercoaster in full swing. It is brilliant. It is the stupidest thing I've ever thought. It excites me. It scares the hell out of me. This baby is bringing out the best and the worst of me all at the same time. This is crazy. I get out of the bed and tip toe downstairs to get my cell phone off the charger. I take it into the garage and call Beth.

This is often how our relationship works, reminiscent of the years she spent in medical school, awake for two or three days at a time. Knowing that I wasn't much of a sleeper, she would call me on her breaks and we would talk things out in the "wee hours" of the morning.

"Beth?" I say her name before she incoherently answers and she knows that it's me.

"Hey, girl. Everything okay?" She sounds sleepy. Medical school was a long time ago.

"Yes. Well, no. I'm not sure."

"Is it one of the girls?" I feel bad. Why do we always think when the phone rings in the middle of the night that the worst has happened? Probably because under normal conditions, non-emergency calls shouldn't be made when people are asleep.

"No, no, nothing like that. It's me. This whole thing; quitting my job, looking for the next thing, wondering where I'm going from here. It's just unnerving, you know? I'm having trouble sleeping."

"Yeah, well it is pretty scary." I know she is struggling to be nice even though the grogginess in her voice tells me she was in a deep sleep.

"I'm sorry to wake you, Beth. Go back to sleep." What was I thinking?

"I couldn't do it." She is waking up. "Don't have the courage." Getting past the four-word sentences. "But trust me, sweetheart, if anyone can figure this out, it's you."

"I'm not so sure."

"Do you realize everybody's waiting to see what you do next? It's like we can live vicariously through you." While I'm sure she meant this as a compliment, this comment touches a nerve. Why do I have to be the one to do the hard stuff?

"You're making me nervous. Too much pressure," I say, regretting having made this call. Why did I call her? I hate her.

"It's not pressure. It's faith. In you. Where's yours?" Silence.

She's right, you know. Trust me.

I'm trying to trust the voice, but let's face it, it's only a voice.

"So talk to me. What are you thinking?" Okay, so I don't really hate her. Truth is, Beth is the only one I know who might truly understand.

"Well, actually, I have this idea. I haven't told anyone about it, and it's in no way fleshed out yet, but it won't let me go." I wonder if Beth will get it. I experience a twist in my gut. I need to protect the blossoming idea, not expose it before it's ready, as if it might shrivel up in the sunlight.

"Are you ready to share it?" God bless Beth.

I decide, right then and there, to take the leap. I tell Beth what I've been thinking, where it has come from, where it might lead. It is kind of weird having the words actually come out of my mouth. I feel completely exposed and vulnerable, but at the same time I feel excitement building up as I talk about it. I don't give Beth a chance to respond; I just keep talking. When I finish, I have poured out my soul and am completely spent and empty.

"Whoa," she says. I brace myself. "That's cool. One thing I know for sure, your voice lit up when you started to talk about it. It's almost like I was listening to a different person. And anything that brings that out in you has got to be right. Follow your gut, sweetie. You have a really good gut," she pauses, "most of the time."

We laugh together, remembering our past adventures. I realize then that I have called Beth for a specific reason; I know she will support me. She always has. And what I need right at this moment is someone who is going to love my baby, just like me, no matter what. I love Beth.

"So what's next?"

"I don't know. I was thinking of maybe calling this guy Mike Johnson. He used to work with me, but I heard that now he advises start up companies or something. I'm thinking he can at least point me in the right direction."

"You know, this may sound a little weird, but maybe it's time for you to just throw out your questions to the universe, then just wait for the answers to come to you."

Beth had recently started practicing with a holistic medical group and since she made that move, she'd been into this spiritual, talk-to-the-universe type of stuff. Well, that's not really fair. Beth was always into some New Agey thing, yoga, meditation, and tarot cards. I always found it amazing because, had she not gone into medicine, she'd truly be vibing off the planet. But it was in the healing with her hands on a physical level that she remained connected to the earth. Years of working in an emergency room kept her grounded in reality on a daily basis. I remember, when she told me she was joining the holistic group, I knew it was the right place for her to be. She could be the next Deepak.

"And what if there's no answer? What if there's silence?" I had tried this throw-your-question-to-the-universe process before. The universe has a tendency to be coy with me.

"Keep listening and wait. Remember, where's your faith, darlin'?" Good question.

Well the bottom line is that I can't do this on my own. I am going to need money and connections with people who can help make it happen. But I know, not everyone will be as easy as Beth. She is biased. She is my best friend.

I have to come up with a way to show this to people, to describe it so that they will be as excited about it as I am. All those things I'd learned in Corporate America need to kick in again: planning, marketing, and researching. I decide to pull together a little presentation. The trick at this point is to infuse the story with everything positive about this idea, everything I love about it. I have to see it in its full glory, to feel it, to live it from the inside out and work backwards from that vision. Sometimes hard questions start to pop into my head; sometimes just ugly negative comments.

I force myself to push the negativity aside. I promise I will deal with each disapproving comment individually, but not now, later. In fact, as they slip into my thoughts, I write them down on a yellow Post It and put it in a box to be dealt with later. These include some serious questions that needed answering: Can you make money off this thing? What don't you know? Do you know anyone who could help you with what you don't know?

And they include some of my basic insecurities: You'd better try to get another job fast before there's a big hole in your resume.

Anything that doesn't give me a feeling of hope and excitement gets thrown into the Post It box. As I write, I can feel the energy building. Pictures are forming in my head. The process helps me channel any kind of doubt in another direction and keeps this baby pure, unadulterated, innocent, big, beautiful, full of hope, bursting with potential, ready to change the world.

So, until now I've had nothing but a concept. But as I sit and put pen to paper, I start to really see it. It is perfect, everything I need it to be. This product is all about helping women to do a lot of the things life requires, but doesn't give us enough time to do with charm, finesse, and confidence. It's portable, it's smart, it solves a major problem.

I clearly don't have all the answers to the questions about how to make it happen. But here's what I do know, I know the feeling of finally understanding something that has always eluded me. It is a great feeling, and that is the feeling I want every woman to have. Imagine if people could feel that way? That would be truly awesome.

Morning Sickness

When old and new try to occupy the same space, the difference is palpable, and uncomfortable. The best cure for morning sickness is to make a commitment, take clear, specific action, and stay focused on what you are trying to create. You are in no way an idle vehicle or unchanging catalyst. You will come out of this a different person than when you began. The transition, though sometimes painful, is necessary for you to develop the strength and acquire the qualities that you will need on the other side where a new reality awaits.

****

"In women who experience morning sickness, symptoms peak precisely when embryonic organ development is most susceptible to chemical disruption. Though the exact mechanisms or causes of morning sickness are still not known, doctors assert it to be a combination of more than one factor. Physiological changes, chemical changes, higher levels of hormones, higher sensitivity, pressure on the stomach are all responsible for causing morning sickness."

Jou Jou Babies

CHAPTER 6

Now that Franklin and the girls are on board, there are so many things to do. I am touched by the support they all have given in their individual age-appropriate ways. Franklin not only steps in to assume household responsibilities, but he is my sounding board for reasonableness. His industry knowledge and connections from writing so many business articles also comes in handy. Dee helps me sometimes with Internet research, Kelli reads aloud descriptive briefs that I write, and Brandy keeps me smiling.

I am in an active phase and happy to feel like I'm doing something. I was always a list maker, so I separate the things I have to do into actions, resources, and information. I am approaching this just like I do every other project I have taken on. I'm grateful that I'm at a point that I know what to do. This is more the old me, but in service to my own calling, my own vision. It is Saturday, and I decide to let the kids sleep in. I head out to the computer store to check out the latest in financial software. While engrossed in the back of the package, a familiar voice interrupts me.

"Well now, how long has it been?" It was Brian Cabu, my old boss.

His presence and his question catch me off guard. I feel like he is still measuring things in an earlier version of time. Truth is, I am in my fourth month, but time has shifted. Months, days, and hours are difficult to count. I have adjusted to this new perspective, although at first it was difficult. When things are cloudy, time slows down. And yet, in a moment of clarity it's as if things happen immediately, fall right into place exactly the way they're supposed to. It is difficult to answer him.

"Not long at all, Brian. How's business?"

"Well, you know, some things never change. We're in the midst of a replan and need to find some money to make sure it's a success, you know. We promoted Joe Martin. Was he there before you left? Do you remember him? He's doing extremely well." Knife in back, turn sharply. "And what are you up to these days?"

"Oh, I'm working on a few business ideas." Okay, so it was only one idea.

"Really? Entrepreneurial dreams. Those kinds of things are risky, you know?"

"I've got some investors willing to take a chance." Okay, so it wasn't really an investor, just a friend who I was going to have dinner with. At least when I ask him, I think he'll agree to have dinner with me. So I exaggerate a little.

"I know some head hunters. I'll give them your name just in case. Anyway, I hope your business idea works out." No he doesn't. He hopes I fall flat on my face. Stupid jerk.

I will not let him get to me. *I will not let him get to me!* I check my watch. "Oh my gosh, I'm so late for an appointment. Take care, Brian." I hold it together while I pay for my things, but once outside the exit door, I lean against the wall where he can't see me and try to catch my breath.

On my way back home the skies open up. The rain falls heavily and soaks the ground so thoroughly that mud and dirt float in pools of brown water all over my front lawn. At home everyone is still asleep on this lazy Saturday morning, and I continue to find it hard to breathe. Once again, I am on some kind of bipolar rollercoaster. I was so excited about this yesterday, and now my heart feels like an anchor has been slip knotted around its thickest part.

What have I done? I drag myself to the coffee pot and pass the pictures of the girls on the piano. Dee would be looking at college soon. And if her mother wasn't such a selfish idiot, she would be able to go to any college her little heart desired. Instead, let's pray she gets some kind of scholarship.

I make a cup of coffee and sit in my usual chair to read the paper. Front-page business section, there is a picture of a woman who graduated from school with me. She is getting some huge promotion at some zillion-dollar investment firm, and they list the range of her salary. Gagging, I spit my coffee out. I don't suppose I will ever make this kind of money in my life; not anymore anyway.

This isn't going to work. Maybe it's time to put my tail between my legs and go back to doing what I know how to do. What in the world made me think this was a good move? At what point does a dream become a fantasy? At what point does persistence become stupidity? Is this the time to come to my senses?

But then I remember the projects that I have seen through to completion, the big ones and the small ones, some for myself, some for others. Some took months to actually get started. I had to think about them for a long time before I actually made the moves to get engaged, to get them to a more active place in my mind. And I try to remember the moment of truth. There was always a turning point of sorts; a point where I finally said okay, enough thinking about this, enough baby steps. And it wasn't until that point that I finally claimed it.

What we do not claim remains invisible.

Didn't I hear that somewhere before? That is the answer; I haven't really claimed this one yet. I need to get to the point where I am willing to tell people this is what I do. And even if they laugh their heads off, I don't care because I am driven by a force that they cannot possibly understand. I get this sudden urge to start cleaning again, but then I realize I have to get to the point where I am no longer cleaning out the old stuff, no longer considering what I have left behind, but focusing instead on where I am going. I realize there is a pivotal point where going back is just as hard, if not harder, than pushing forward to the other side.

I think back on everything that has happened so far, and I realize that I am a completely different person than I was the day I walked out of that office. And regardless of the outcome, this child, this pregnancy, has changed me. To abort at this point is not an option.

C'mon. Just claim me.

I have to take the next step and that will be the point of no return. The step that truly involves someone else. The step that forces me to take another one because there are others involved now and if I don't do what I've committed to do, I look like a complete idiot; good old accountability doing what it does best. It is time to move out of that comfortable phase of dreaming and choosing and playing around with all the possibilities. It is time to make a decision. It is time put a stake in the ground. It is time to move forward.

This is a crucial step. And, in some ways, it is a painful step. But now that I've made up my mind to take it, I feel a whole lot better than I did an hour ago.

Fetal Development

You're showing. And it's time to share your idea pregnancy
with the world so that people don't think you're just fat. At
this stage you must call on your network and be prepared to
have your baby shaken, stirred, and turned on its head. Not
to worry, you have already protected it through its most
vulnerable stages. You've developed the skill of hearing
what needs to be heard and letting go of what needs to go.
At this point, the harder the questions and the broader the
input, the better. Be prepared that at the end of this phase
the idea may look different than when you started. It will
have adjusted to the environment and acquired the
necessary qualities for survival. And so have you.

"Already your baby has the foundation for thought, senses, feeling, and more! Heart and primitive circulatory system rapidly form. While still in its beginning stages, this is the very life support system that will carry your child throughout his or her life."
The Heart of an Embryo

CHAPTER 7

I purposely stayed away from my traditional navy blue suits and pumps. Just like when I was part of the corporate world it meant everything to fit in, now that I have made such a deliberate step outside of the circle, it is equally important that I don't fit in. I need to represent quirkiness and creativity. I have to be willing to position myself as the one who just couldn't be held down, couldn't be constrained.

I had asked Mike Johnson to meet me for drinks, told him that I had an idea that I was playing around with and wanted his opinion. I chose Mike for specific reasons. First of all, he knows me well enough to know that I'm not some kind of flake. Mike and I grew up together in an earlier corporate playground. We had a special relationship and had always kept in touch. Unlike many of my other peers, there never seemed to be competition between us.

Back then, I had shared with him an outline that I used for performance reviews and I believe he was genuinely grateful. I'm hoping he feels he owes me one. On the other hand, he doesn't know me well enough to be biased by our friendship. I need a neutral observer. I don't want anyone who either loves me or hates me to be the first whom I officially present to. I am beyond the realm of protection. I want someone who will give me honest feedback and who has no stake, personal or otherwise, in whether I succeed or fail.

"Wow! You look great!" He says as he stands and uncomfortably wavers between shaking my hand and hugging me. Good. The printed skirt and long earrings worked.

"Thanks, Michael. You look wonderful, too." I'm lying. He looks old. Mike had stayed in that first company for his entire corporate career. He left a few years ago after cashing in on some lucrative investments. From what I heard, he was doing really well as an angel investor.

"It's funny, after you called I spoke to someone else from your old company. A guy named Joe Martin. Do you know him?" You mean Joe the idiot, dimwit who convinced my boss that he could double the price of one of our products and still sell enough to make a plan? The Joe whom they promoted after decimating a perfectly good business? That Joe?

"Yes. I know Joe," I say, with an innocent smile that can easily be interpreted as fond remembrance. "How's he doing anyway?"

"Well, he's got some idea of his own that he's trying to launch." I wonder if Brian Cabu knows that. I want to tell Michael that investing in anything that Joe is involved in is a big mistake, but he might think I'm small and bitter.

I make a mental note to tell Michael the truth once we get to know each other better. But for now I just say, "Oh, really?" with my smile still pasted in place.

We spend some time reminiscing about the old days when Michael finally cuts to the chase. "So what's this new idea you have?"

It is an interesting feeling of nervous excitement I have before I start to share it with him. This fluttering in my stomach is almost like a first date. I had tried to prepare myself for every possible outcome. I had gone through with a fine-tooth comb every angle that made sense. I forced myself to go back to my Post It box and deal with every single question, issue, and insecurity until it was resolved. I believe that this is it.

The idea has changed during the course of this process. Some things worked, but I had to let some things go. I had to be brutally honest with every question and be willing to make adjustments. As the idea began to take on its own form, it was different from what I had originally imagined.

Now, I know the intricacies of this product inside and out. Any other product that is remotely like the one I have conceived has been looked at and looked at again. I know what is special about my idea, what makes it different from everyone else's; why it should succeed where others may have failed and why it is even better than those that have succeeded. I know how to price it. I know how to market it. I know how to distribute it. I can't find any holes. As far as I'm concerned, it is absolutely brilliant.

I show him a designed sketch and my financial assumptions. My final words hang inside of an awkward silence. Mike sits there and thinks for a good minute, which in all honesty feels like an eternity; that time thing again. Finally he looks up at me and speaks.

"Well, your passion is impressive." So what is he saying? My baby sucks, but he loves me for loving it? My back goes up in a moment of defensive posturing.

Shut up and listen!

"But you and I both know, passion doesn't pay the bills." He had slipped into a different mode. Mike Johnson was now in a no nonsense zone, analyzing the real potential for this business idea. He was flipping through my financial documents with pure dexterity.

"Having said that, I do think the idea has some merit. I especially like the way you're going to market it. Very innovative. No one has truly tapped into the female marketplace this way. I also like the interactive part of it, although once you start adding the chip technology, it could complicate things. You should actually talk to Joe." I bite my lip. I hope it doesn't bleed. "His idea used some kind of microprocessor, too. Different type of application, but I'll be honest, his financials were a lot more attractive." No surprise there.

"Aside from that, I have a few other thoughts." Within five minutes I know that I have picked the right person to share my plan with. He is so good. He asks legitimate questions, some I had already considered but obviously hadn't answered sufficiently; others, to be honest, I had never even thought about. Questions about product quality, pricing, and a potential hole in my distribution strategy. He even recommends a person from IT who would be great in helping me set up the infrastructure I would need.

He thinks out loud. "This is interesting. I hope you can make it happen."

"Would you be willing to invest in it?" I brace myself. This is the ultimate question.

"If you can answer those questions to my satisfaction, I'd be willing to hear your pitch. But, I'll be honest, you've got some work to do. And some stiff competition. I've got a lot being presented to me these days and sometimes it just boils down to making a choice, you know?" Okay, that's honest. Not exactly what I want to hear, but honest.

Be grateful. Better now than later.

It is done. The first hint of exposure to the real world and my budding creation has passed the test. Yes, there's definitely more development to go through. We are nowhere close to being ready for the world yet, but I know I have something that is strong and can survive. I walk out of the restaurant with a little extra pep in my step. Like a woman who has been hiding her secret of being with child, I realize I must be starting to show. It is obvious that I am

carrying something within me, but somehow it feels
extremely light.

Sharing Space

The expansion needed to share space with a big idea feels like it could actually cause one to explode. You are stretching beyond normal proportions and while you are fully engaged it is important to remain grounded. Think about your fertile ground of discontent and make sure you're not repeating the same mistakes over again. This time you have the ability to create what you want, so be sure you make enough room to accommodate it all. An influx of new energy, be it money, fame, or the manifestation of a new idea requires a spiritual expansion large enough to hold it.

"As we turn the corner of the final phase, preparations are being made for birth. At this point there is a change in the fetal activity, a conflict of sorts, as strong activity is confined within the restriction of a mother's womb. Contractions are soon to begin as the baby desires its own space, its own breath, and its own life."
The Miracle of Life

CHAPTER 8

How incredible to be able to expand, to incorporate this new life within me without completely rupturing. Everything within me is stretching. Will I ever be normal size again? There are days it drains me completely, a parasite taking nourishment from me in this crazy zero sum game. I am literally the arms and legs of a new being, and it has virtual control over me in a physical way.

I am barely thinking, just doing; so many things that my old rational, reasonable self would never consider doing. But I don't even stop to ask, much less answer, any questions. I simply follow what I am told to do. I am exhausted.

Lately, however, the relationship between this baby and me has crossed an interesting boundary. It's not so painful, so draining. It's a partnership now that has taken a symbiotic turn. I need it as much as it needs me. Gradually I learn how to gain strength from it. I feel as if I live in different ether, like I exist in a place where I can see things differently, hear things differently.

Newly developed antennae allow me to pick up on sights, sounds, and signals that otherwise would have gone unnoticed. I must be glowing. I'm certain it appears that way on the outside because I am carrying something special on the inside. I have changed. I see it now so clearly; what I want, what I need, what needs to happen. And so it is.

"Hey, I'm going out with the girls for some ice cream. Want to come?" What a perfect thing to do on a Sunday afternoon. Franklin is so good at impromptu family moments. If I hadn't been so consumed with my latest addition, I might actually consider it.

But things are starting to come together. I have the initial designs. The costs are still pretty high, but I just had a conversation with the chip manufacturer, and there might be a way to use a smaller microprocessor, which would work just fine overall, but would take significant costs out of the system. I have scheduled some groups of women in my target audience to come by the house this week and I'm going to expose them to a concept and early prototype, see what they think. I want everything to be ready for that.

In the meantime, Mike Johnson has invited me to a meeting. He has pulled together a tribune of his four partners, each wanting to invest in the next big idea and wants to know if I'm ready to pitch my idea to a bigger audience for some seed money. I really want that seed money.

"Can you bring me something back? A cone or something would hit the spot right about now."

"No," he answers curtly. He is kidding, right? "I was going to take them down by lake and sit and eat there. If we got you something, it would melt." So, he is serious. I can't believe he isn't going to bring me back some ice cream. And what's with this big old sarcastic chip on his shoulder?

"Never mind." I don't want to hear what he's mad about.

"You know, I've been taking Kelli to her book club. It's actually kind of fun being the only Dad there." A pang of familiar hurt hits me hard.

"Oh, yeah. Did Matilda get adopted yet?" My proof that I wasn't too far behind in the story.

"Babe, we finished Matilda months ago. You would know that if you were ever here anymore." I set myself up for that one.

"Franklin, please don't start. I have thirty people coming over to view this in a few days and I don't have time to argue with you right now."

"You? No time? Well, there's a big surprise." He's starting to squint at me. Why is he so mad?

"What's that supposed to mean?"

"Hey, you know what? Just do what you have to do." He starts to walk away.

"What's *that* supposed to mean?" He is really pissing me off.

"I mean exactly what I said. I can't believe I actually thought that once you quit the corporate gig you'd be here more. Not just physically, but emotionally, too. What a joke."

"Oh my God! Grow up, Franklin! I'm trying to make something happen here, and all you're thinking about is yourself.

"Myself and those three girls out there who barely remember what it's like to spend time with their mother."

"That's not fair."

"At least when you could blame it on your job, you'd apologize every so often. Now, you're not even sorry. You enjoy not being here. All this work to save the world and you can't even hold on to your own family. Have fun, sweetheart. We'll see you when we get back. I guess." He slams the door before I can respond with a good come back.

I spend the next ten minutes pacing, throwing things, and talking to myself. You'd think he'd be supportive. You'd think he'd be excited about what I'm doing. I try to remember. He was supportive for a while. Very supportive. When did it stop?

I've been at this for eight months now. All through the initial design and conceptual work, he was right there with me. I can't figure out when I lost him. Maybe it was when he was working on that tablet technology article and he was almost late with his submission because I dropped Brandy off with him while I met with that supplier.

Or was it his piece on the car industry? Both seemed like a long time ago. I used to always know the topic of the articles Franklin was working on. But I have no idea what he is writing about now. I have no idea what book the book club is reading.

Somewhere in the recesses of my being I know he is right. How did I become so distant? I look out the window and see all four of them hanging out by the water with cones in hand. Franklin and Dee are in a deep and seemingly very adult conversation.

The point of this was never to lose what I had. I clearly had not made enough space for the new arrival. I think about it. I can push the groups back for a week or two. Nothing is really rushing me. After all, I'm the boss, right? I grab my jacket and head toward the lake to be with my family.

I'm sitting outside of Mike Johnson's office talking with Millie, the woman who answers his phone, keeps his calendar, and otherwise controls his life. She is funny. I'm nervous, though. There are three other people with prototypes and PowerPoint presentations vying for some financial backing for their own respective brainchildren. Millie's phone rings and I know that they are summoning us. I start to gather my stuff and in walks Joe Martin. He has a presentation of his own. This man has come to represent my official corporate nemesis.

"Okay, everyone, Mr. Johnson and his team will see you now." I realize that we are all presenting at the same time. I didn't realize that's how these things worked. Millie winks at me and mouths the words *good luck* before the door closes behind us.

Mike is sitting on one side of a large dark wood conference table. He is with three other guys, all of whom look like cool people. None look terribly comfortable in a suit. There is also a woman on their side of the table. She is gorgeous and had clearly spent a lot of money on her simple black dress that flows in all the right places.

"Good afternoon, everyone." Mike is clearly the leader of this process. "We don't always do it this way, having everybody in here at the same time, but we've signed confidentiality agreements here, and we happen to have a group of projects with little overlap in the competitive marketplace. It saves a lot of time if you don't have to come in and set up separately. Plus, sometimes it gives us an opportunity to learn from each other."

We all continue to set up as he speaks. I have one eye on Joe the entire time I set up my presentation. There once was a time when his presence would have disturbed me to my core. In fact, those old feelings almost start to overtake me. But then I catch myself. I realize Joe Martin is searching for something, just like I am. And I don't have the heart to be mad at him for that. The other stuff--the integrity of his idea, the accuracy of his numbers--I truly know nothing about that. That is between him and whatever God he answers to. In my mind, I wish him well and let him go.

While we set up, the investment team is joking and playing around. It's obvious they are comfortable with each other. They can afford to be comfortable. They are rich, and nobody is about to pass judgment on their creative offspring in the next couple of hours.

Joe goes first. I can't focus on what his product is. I just keep wondering if he still has a job at the old company. My ears perk up when I hear him mention the same chip that I will be using in my product. I had researched this chip extensively and it was perfect for my product, but it certainly wasn't perfect for everything. In fact, Franklin and I had a long conversation about the various manufacturers and their areas of expertise.

Honestly, Joe is doing a really good job. The investors ask him some fairly pointed questions and he seems to know all the answers. He always did.

Then Michael starts pushing him. "Joe, I don't know if you saw this article in last week's *Business Week*. The micro-processing chip that you're using was rated fairly low when it came to simultaneous multiple usages. It says the speed becomes a real bottle neck under the wrong conditions." Joe tries to cover it, but I can tell he has never seen this article. Michael starts reading from it verbatim and, sure enough, the way Joe was planning on using this chip was exactly the way it was *not* meant to be used. I am not the least bit surprised. That's the problem with being a charmer like Joe Martin. He can get really far without a lot of follow up.

There are two other presentations before mine. On the one hand, I am nervous. On the other, I know exactly what I am doing.

I wave to Millie on my way out the door. All the presenters are now feeling much more relaxed and we wish each other luck as we head toward the elevator. There were some good ideas presented and, since our products are so different in nature, we see no risk in being nice to each other; except for Joe Martin. He is not a happy camper. As the door slams behind him I have a strong feeling that I will never see him again.

I stop and buy *Business Week* at a newsstand before getting into my car. I load all my stuff and, before pulling out of the parking lot, I search through the magazine. There it is, the write-up on the microprocessor marketplace and competitive strengths and weaknesses. The byline: Franklin Moore, my husband.

Breathe

Contractions

The pain is startling, catching you off guard. Could it be?
Are you ready? And then it strikes again, this time more
directly, with more certainty. You are definitely on the
verge of something bigger than ever before. And in that
moment of ultimate transition, you breathe life into
something new with such strength and determination that it
can now breathe on its own. It has become...Real.

****

"During active labor, your cervix begins to dilate more rapidly and contractions are longer, stronger, and closer together. People often refer to the last part of active labor as 'transition'. This is when you may begin to lose faith in your ability to handle the pain, so you'll need lots of extra encouragement and support from those around you. It may be useful to focus on the fact that those hard contractions are helping your baby make the journey out into the world."

BabyCenter.com

CHAPTER 9

So much has happened since I got the first go ahead. Mike actually only gave me half of what I needed, so I had to pitch this to other investors to make up the difference. At this point I just need enough to produce a decent prototype, get some real feedback from my consumer, and pull together a big event to raise the real dollars for the first production run and all that I will need to launch this in a bigger way.

Many have said no. But it's funny, earlier in this pregnancy a "no" would have sent me into a melodramatic tailspin. Now, it's just part of the process. See, I've had enough successes to know I've really got something here. I try to think of the setbacks as guidance. Every one of them has led me to make adjustments, sometimes to what I'm creating, sometimes to myself. Either way, we both come out with movement of some kind. And I get better and better at making the movement forward, not backwards.

I finally get approval for the other half of the seed money, from a friend of a friend of a friend. She seems excited about what I'm trying to do and tells me about all the other successful investments she's made, some of which I have heard of, some, not a clue. She is different from Michael, though, and something about that bothers me a little. She just didn't ask the same kinds of questions he did.

It feels good to be so totally engaged with something that I believe so strongly in. I find a designer and an engineer to build the prototype, and I give them clear directions about what I'm trying to do. They both get it all wrong.

They unveil, with pride, their own personal children, but certainly not mine. When I see the final version of my vision that I thought I had described with such infinite detail, I grab the arm of my Grandmother's chair and sit slowly and carefully. I try to come up with the words that will get us back on track without hurting their feelings. I open my mouth and start to cry.

"What? You don't like it?" Christopher is my designer. "You've got to be kidding. This is a beautiful piece of work."

"I thought it would be smaller."

"Smaller? We can make it smaller. Is that the only problem?" He is clearly getting angry.

"And lighter, and more funky, you know? Trendy, hip, with it." I'm whining now, I know. But I can't help it.

"Trendy? Hip? What the hell are you talking about?" Christopher has clearly had it with me.

"And I didn't think it would be so complicated. I wanted simple." There were so many things wrong I didn't know where to begin.

"Complicated? Don't be ridiculous! It's exactly what you described." What is so hard about this project? How could his interpretation be so far off from what I had seen in my head?

Obviously, it is me. Maybe it isn't so bad. Maybe I can work with it.

Christopher puts his coat on, picks up his designs, and walks toward the door. "Don't think you're getting away without paying me for this. I gave you a discount to start with, but this meeting is full cost. I'll send you my bill." The door slams solidly behind him.

"So, that went well." I look at Gina the programmer I hired who specialized in interactivity. Thank God she hasn't left yet. "I'm sorry, Gina, it's just not what I expected. Just give me a minute and let me see if I can figure out what went wrong." The first contraction; that burst of pain so sharp and so hard that it actually comes from out of nowhere. I'm not sure what it is, but I know it's different than any other pain I've ever felt before.

Breathe.

Fortunately, Gina and I are closer in our understanding of how this should work. There are some discrepancies, but we talk them through. She goes off with a direction that seems new to her, but is what I thought I had said in the first place.

****

I have been planning my big unveiling event for next month. The plan is to invite all the people I know who have an interest in what I'm doing, especially those who have money. I am going to need some serious investors in this project, and I have to get them as excited about this as I am. The science museum is a perfect location, filled with the work of the most brilliant minds in history. They rent it out on weekday evenings for parties and entertainment. I stop at the museum on my way home and as I pull up to the parking lot I see the news cameras set up outside of the building, several feet back from the steps that lead to the entryway.

As I get closer, the vision of what had happened starts to take form. The gray concrete floor outside of the building has huge cracks in it that had buckled and lifted from the ground. Yellow caution tape is stretched across the cracks in the ground. To the right, men are standing knee deep in water with boots that come up to their knees. They tread through the water with heavy feet sloshing and pull up large piles of sandy mud with shovels.

"Water main break." Someone from the crowd that had started to gather around felt it appropriate to explain to me.

"I see that."

"They say there are sections inside that are totally ruined. Say it could shut down the museum for three or four months."

I feel a sudden twisting in my gut.

Breathe!

"Excuse me?"

"The check bounced. I didn't stutter." Christopher will never forgive me.

"I don't understand. I deposited that weeks ago. Let me call you back, Christopher."

"Yeah, call me back. I'll have my lawyer on hold." I start to curse at him. Never mind.

I call the bank, and I get Maria, lovely woman who helped me set up the account and even had given me some loan advice.

"I was about to call you." Something in her voice did not sound good; not good at all. That check you placed, the one from Hendle and Associates," she carefully pauses, "It didn't clear." So the friend of a friend of a friend was obviously a fraud. Maria waits as if she is expecting me to scream or maybe die. I consider both.

"Okay." I say this very slowly, trying to regroup my thoughts.

"I checked into the company for you. Turns out they are filing Chapter 11."

"Bankruptcy?"

"Yeah. Something about a lawsuit with one of their products that proved to be a fire hazard. They lost the case and owe lots of money in damages."

"When did this happen?" I try to make sense of this in my mind.

"The charges were filed a couple of months ago, but it was resolved last week. There's nothing in that account. The check is no good," Maria says, anticipating some eruption.

"But I've already spent that money." Clearly, I'm not understanding this.

She responds slowly, enunciating every word as if I was mentally challenged, "There's no money to have spent."

"I can't believe they didn't even call me to tell me."

"Some of the principals can't even be found. It's not a good situation, honey."

I hang up the phone too stunned to be angry. I knew it. The red flag had gone off in my head, but I wanted so badly for this woman to be legit, I didn't listen. It is over. Nothing is finished, I am in serious debt, and now a good chunk of what I thought I had simply does not exist. It is definitely over. It is time to cry uncle.

That really is the ultimate question. I have this dream. I push on it and push on it, overcoming all the obstacles, jumping through every hoop. When is it time to throw in the proverbial towel?

My cell phone rings. It's Jolie.

"Hey, I just got off the phone with the museum. The head of reservations is a friend of mine, and we figured out a way to reroute traffic so that they never see the water main flooding. There's another area in the east wing that wasn't damaged at all and it can fit our event. It's cheaper, too." Jolie has been so good helping me pull this together. Here is where her A-type personality, combined with Brenda's serious connections throughout the museum network, came in handy. She was almost as excited about this as I was. I don't know how to tell her.

"It's over, Jolie."

"Beg your pardon?"

"One of my main investors just filed Chapter 11 and can't be found. I'm finished."

Silence.

"Okay, there has to be way to handle this." Jolie isn't ready to cry uncle.

"Jolie, did you hear what I said? It's over. There's nothing left."

"You mean to tell me that with all the work and heart and energy you put into this thing, you're actually going to give up now?" she pushes back.

"I don't exactly have a choice."

"There's always a choice."

"No, there isn't. Sometimes there's only one option, and it's not the one you want."

"You don't believe that. I know you don't believe that. I'll be the first to admit I wasn't crazy about this from the beginning, but, dammit, you proved me wrong. You've been like the Energizer bunny with this thing, and you're so close. It's brilliant, darlin'. It's truly brilliant. You can't give up now."

I remember nine months ago when I first told Jolie that I had left my job. How far she had come. "There's a fine line between brilliance and insanity."

"Don't you dare say that to me. Don't you dare! There's always more than one option. You taught me that. You showed me that! So one investor proved worthless. There are others. There's loans and credit. Put your money where your heart is, sweetie. What exactly are you willing to give up here?" Jolie surprises me with her persistence.

"I can't give anymore, Jolie. I'm done."

She hangs up on me and I don't even care. There is a strange sense of surrealism around me, almost like the air is super thick. I hear my family in the background carrying on with life as if that phone call had never happened. Franklin peeks his head in, a strange déjà vu from another place, another time.

"Hey. Are you okay?" I can't even answer him.

"What? Tell me what. Did somebody die?" What an interesting question. I guess in some ways this was like a stillborn birth. They had funerals for that, didn't they?

"Just the business. Nobody important." I tell him what has happened and he sits, stunned. There is an awkward silence in our kitchen. We are both afraid to speak. Dee walks in with the day's mail and throws it on the table in front of Franklin. She is rambling on about some teenage problem, but I honestly can't translate the words in my head. Eventually she feels the heaviness in the room.

"What's going on?"

Soon Kelli comes in, holding Brandy's tiny hand, not wanting to miss anything. As soon as they open the door, they are both too smart to say anything. Brandy climbs into my lap and lays her head on my chest. I hug her tightly. The kitchen remains silent with an awkward kind of calm. For some reason, Franklin picks up the top letter and opens it. It is a familiar marketing letter pre-approving us for a zero percent interest credit card for eighteen months.

"Didn't you once tell me zero percent interest is like free money?" Franklin asks.

"Sort of. You still have to pay it back."

"Hell, you'd have to pay back the crooked angel investors too, wouldn't you?" There is a dim light bulb starting to shine above his head.

"Well, yeah. But it's different. They're betting on the success of the business."

"So are we," he says, with that devilish charming smile.

I look at him and can't believe he's suggesting this. It actually could work. We start rummaging through the mail to see if anyone else is willing to pre-approve us for a low interest loan. The kids join in, not sure what they're looking for, but grateful for the break in awkward, deadening silence.

Breathe! Push!

Delivery

Had you known about the dragons before the journey
began, you might never have packed the bag and started the
journey. But the wonderful 20/20 vision of reflection and
hindsight reveals the true nature of the birth of a brilliant
idea. Focus your energy, conjure up big, bold impossible
images, and hold on to them tight. This is how we press the
vision through our fully dilated individual birth canals, at
which point our precious young idea takes on a life of its
own.

****

"While the fetus is in the womb, it breathes by exchanging oxygen and carbon dioxide through the mother's circulation via the placenta. Once the umbilical cord is cut and the baby takes the first breath, the lungs inflate and begin working on their own. It sounds like a gasp, as the newborn's central nervous system reacts to the sudden change in temperature and environment."

MedLine Plus

CHAPTER 10

I want everything to be perfect, but at this point, I have long since given up thinking I am in control here. I have been up most of the night setting everything up. Brenda continued to push her connections with museum management, and they have allowed us to set up our dais and table right across from the Marie Curie exhibit, which faced the latest Einstein exhibit. Location, location, location.

I had drawings prepared of the concept for our product, and they were displayed on easels throughout the space. After losing Christopher, I revised my product description and the idea articulation. I included drawings and color palettes to bring more clarity to what I was thinking. I found another designer, Jo Jo, who was able to develop the prototype at almost half the cost and was an absolute joy to work with, and who "got me." It made all the difference in the world. Jo Jo made a wonderful prototype of the product, which we planned on demonstrating during the presentation. It was beautifully mounted next to the conceptual drawings.

Jolie insisted that I make a real entrance, so I promised I wouldn't arrive at the actual unveiling until everyone else was there, mingling, observing, and talking among themselves.

I stand now in front of the mirror. All of my normal support systems are already at the museum. For the moment, I am on my own. Franklin had helped me decide on this gorgeous golden gown that was just perfect. I had my hair done earlier this afternoon and did the standard manicure pedicure, more to relax than anything else. As I turn and see my reflection in the mirror, I am taken aback.

Tonight, I look physically different, remnants of a previous me, but rearranged somehow, like the photo had been retouched. Smoother, more relaxed, a hint of a glow. I know the relaxed part has nothing to do with getting more sleep. Truth is, I am exhausted, yet, in some strange way, I am energized. I take a moment, here in the quiet of my empty home, standing here in front of the mirror in my fullest self and take a long, deep breath. In that moment, I realize how far I have come in nine months.

You done good, kiddo.

Even the whisper was different. There were hints of its original tonality, but now it was deeper, richer, more defined, more specific.

Let's go present me to the world.

"Did you check the food? Is it exactly the way we wanted it?" The questions roll off, although I know Beth has everything covered. We walk briskly down the corridor toward the exhibit room, the rhythm of our heels clicking against the marble floor, totally in sync. The air of festivity is increasing exponentially as we get close to the event space. Yesterday this same ballroom foyer contained little more than a dormant lull of expectation. Now it is literally buzzing.

"Yeah. I came by this afternoon and talked with the caterer. He was on top of everything, knew exactly what you wanted. How did you find that guy? Monty. He's great. Really, everything's going to be fine."

I stop and take both of her hands in mine. I feel strongly that she needs to hear me say this. "I don't know what I'd do without you."

"I know," she says, turns me around, and pushes me toward the door.

"How do I look?" Beth plucks an invisible strand of thread from my shoulder.

"Like someone who has no idea of all the crap that led to this moment. You look great. Stop worrying about it."

Beth opens the double doors in an uncharacteristic dramatic gesture, and I am filled with awe. The dais has been set with a flowing gold and white banner stretched across the front of the table with the words "*Introducing*" written across it. Behind the dais, on a marble column stands a giant twenty-foot replica of the brand logo that we created. It was perfect. It represented everything I wanted this business to be. It sits comfortably behind the dais with Athena-like presence.

The open bar has a line of people waiting to be served while the band plays over on the side. Monty is serving horsd'oeuvres from a tray across the room. I catch his eye, and he winks at me. I wink back. Round tables are covered with crisply starched white tablecloths, each with a crystal centerpiece filled with gold and white flowers that stretch dramatically toward the bright fluorescent lights.

"So what do you think?" Beth whispers just behind my head.

"It's beautiful," I say, catching the overwhelming emotion in my voice.

"Takes after its mother." It is Franklin looking incredibly dapper in black tie and tails. I hug him tightly and silently wonder what I ever did to deserve so much love in my life.

Everyone is talking and laughing with drinks in hand. I make sure to touch base with everyone who has come. Some have agreed to function as a mini board of directors while I get this up and running. But the real reason for tonight's event is money. I need to solicit the investment from everyone I know to get this thing off the ground.

I look at Beth and give the signal. It is time for my speech. So much is riding on the next few moments. My ability to convince these people not only to come to my party, eat my food and drink my wine, but generously invest some money in the venture, that is what it all boils down to. After getting everyone's attention, I pull out my speech. As I stand at the podium, I look around the room and take it all in. I realize at this point I have to completely surrender. My work is done. It is time to bring this baby into the world.

When I finish my speech, I literally hold my breath. The applause starts slowly, one person at a time, but then seems to go on for hours. There goes that time thing again. As the rumbling applause continues, I look up and see the twenty-foot logo standing dramatically above me start to wobble, teetering to the rhythm of the standing ovation and, in what seems like slow motion, begin to lose its balance.

In shock and immobile, I cover my head as the giant logo comes tumbling down toward me. The room holds its breath as they all watch in horror as it careens directly targeting my head. It strikes my shoulders with a hollow thud.

As others push their chairs aside, they rush toward me. In a moment, however, they all realize what is happening. The enormous replica hits my back and bounces off, comes down again, and bounces off the head of one of the board members, comes down again, and knocks over several wine glasses on the table.

Light as a feather, the air-filled balloon keeps randomly bumping into things, up and down again until it finally reaches equilibrium across the table. Facing up, it seems quite pleased with its harmless dance as the room exhales and erupts in a burst of laughter.

Legacy

As we drove up to the dormitory, I had such a mix of feelings. It was overwhelming. Franklin let me off in front while he followed the student in the orange vest giving directions as to the best place to park. I was grateful for a moment alone before I faced my oldest daughter. Parents weekend; everyone mulling around reminiscing about the good old days, giving useless advice and direction to young men and women who have since learned to follow their own path. And yet they listened to us, patiently, wondering when they will hear something useful.

In the distance I saw a figure running toward me with her arms outstretched. I knew this couldn't be my Dee. This grown person was awkwardly running, hints of a child in a grown up body. My God, had she changed that much in the two months since college began? Apparently, yes.

"Mommy!" How weird. Over the past two years I had gotten used to her not calling me that in public. Since she turned fifteen it was "Mom," "Ma," or even "Mother" when she attempted to chastise me in her teenage way.

"Dee?" Oh, my God, who was this woman? If she could have, she would have jumped right into my arms. But she was much too big, or maybe I was way too small. Either way, while we may have wanted to merge, it soon became obvious that we both needed to stand on our own, so we just hugged, really hard.

"Goodness, girl. You'd think you had been gone for years."

"So much has happened since I started. Where's Daddy?"

"Parking the car. He said to just meet him at the restaurant."

We walked together, not mother to child, but woman to woman. It felt different, but I forced myself to just flow with it.

"I think I've decided on a major, Mom. Journalism."

Inside, my heart sank. Dee was always so good at math and science. I had always hoped she would go to medical school. I had hoped her strategy to declare an undecided major would lead to something more practical than writing.

Clearly my expression exposed my disappointment. Dee's excitement slowly dissipated.

"All I know is, I'm following your lead here, Mom. You're the one who taught me the whole follow your passion thing. Remember, take risks, do what you love," she said, badly imitating my voice.

"Did I say that?" Great comeback.

"No you *did* that. Oh, my God, Mommy you're like the poster child for *follow your dreams*. We all look to you to see how it's done."

I had to let it go. This was her journey, not mine. And following in her father's writing footsteps made a lot of sense.

"As long as you're happy, sweetie. But where did this come from? I didn't think you liked writing that much."

"Actually, I've been somewhat of a closet writer all along. Never liked to show my work to anybody, you know. But we had these seminars during the first week. Personality tests and stuff like that. They asked me to write about the freshman orientation experience. They published me, Mom! In the campus paper. It was very cool."

What could I say? I admired her desire to find what she loved and her willingness to try. I smiled. It *was* cool. I don't think I'd ever seen Dee quite so excited about anything.

"So how's the business going, Mom?"

"I've decided to sell it."

"Sell it? Why?" It was my turn to be deflated by the disappointment in her voice.

"Because I think I've given it all I can give it. It's time for somebody else to take it to the next level, you know. I've actually been made quite an offer."

"But you're wrapped up in that business, Mom. What are you going to do next?"

"Not really sure. Maybe start up another one. Maybe try something totally different. I'm open to all possibilities."

"Is this what you really want?" I was surprised to see her reaction. I didn't think she cared that much.

"I'm just throwing out possibilities, Dee. One thing leads to another. I mean, I started out wanting to be a CEO of a Fortune 100 company and look where that led me."

"That's what you wanted?"

"Yeah. And before that I wanted to be an engineer and before that a veterinarian and after reading about Harriet in the fourth grade, I wanted to be a spy."

She laughed. "Wow, Mom. I didn't realize you were so flaky."

"As a pie crust." We laughed. "You want to know the real lesson here? To bring all of your self to everything you do and don't get attached to anything. Don't get stuck. Keep on moving. Be grateful for every experience, good and bad, and in the course of it all let it lead you to understanding how *To Be* even more than you were the day before."

My daughter looked at me strangely, and I wasn't sure if she was ready to hear what I had said. But then, I saw a settling, a recognition cross over her face like a sunbeam.

"Maybe you'll come up with some different philosophy, Dee. Just do me favor. Let me know what you find out." We looked up toward the restaurant and saw Franklin standing outside. Arms interlocked, we walked in step towards our respective futures.

Hey let's start working on me*!*

END

Appendix:

Idea Birthing

Key Stages and Questions to Ask

Fertility: Recognize discontent as divine fertile ground.

Key Questions.

So, what situations are you facing right now that could be the basis for your Divine Discontent? Are you focused on the things you *want* to do or just trying to keep your head above water? Are you constantly faced with situations where you think you could do a better job than the person handling it? Does the same frustrating situation keep happening to you over and over again? Do you have a thought or idea that keeps popping into your head that you just can't shake? Do other people take your ideas and try to claim them as their own? How do you wish you could spend your time every day? Is that anything like what you're actually doing? Do you give more to other people's dreams than your own?

DNA: Deliberately develop and contribute your personal DNA.

<u>Key Questions.</u>

Can you remember a time when you felt you could do anything? What did you dream of doing then? When you envision the perfect future, what part do you play? What does that feel like? How is it different from the way you feel now? With friends and family, what role do you typically play? What are you good at? What about your current position do you want to keep and what do you wish you could change? Do you need more knowledge or skills? Is there an efficient way to get them? Do you take the time to savor the moment? Is there consistency among your interests, likes, and hobbies that helps better define who you are and what you want most in life? What is your intention for the life you want to create?

The Perfect Mate: Potent seeds are found in the solution of a bigger problem

<u>Key Questions.</u>

What are some of the things you find most frustrating? Is it just you or do you suspect others have the same frustration? Can you imagine what would need to happen to eliminate that frustration? Does the solution seem too far-fetched? If so, can it be broken down into smaller pieces? Are you always on the lookout for problems to solve? Do you have ideas that were crushed before you had a chance to think them through? Do you have a cadre of "small" ideas that solve a real problem? Can you recognize good ideas? How do they make you feel? What makes them good? Can you feel a real opportunity starting to surface?

Conception: Clarity emerges from the fusion of your gifts with the needs of others.

Key Questions.

Are you open to the unexpected? Are you starting to see your idea more clearly? Can you feel it? Does it solve an important problem? Does it capitalize on your unique gifts and talents? Can you clearly articulate the bencfit your idea provides? Can you support that with a credible and valid reason why? Does it feel like it makes perfect sense? Do you wonder why no one has ever thought of it before?

Embryonic Development: Nurture and protect, share sparingly and listen for guidance.

Key Questions.

What kind of support do you have? Have you found the person, group, or community that will support and encourage without unnecessary criticism? Are you listening? Paying attention? Do you have specific questions? Can you formulate them in your mind and listen for answers, even in places you don't expect them? Have you captured any viable negative thoughts in a central place to be dealt with later? Have you created something physical to represent your idea; a simple model, a drawing, a Power Point presentation? Have you started to notice thoughts and ideas that confirm your direction; articles, songs, random conversations?

Morning Sickness: Make a commitment and take clear specific action.

Key Questions.

Are you still questioning? Have you fully accepted that this is something that you're going to do? Can you still be hurt by negative comments or can you take what's useful and throw the rest away? Are you ready to do the hard work? Have you developed a plan? Do you have resources that can help you? Do you know what you need? Do you know what you know? Do you know what you don't know? Are you ready?

Fetal Development: Establish your network, encourage input and address every issue surfaced.

Key Questions.

Have you identified and contacted your key resources? Are they neutral people with no vested interest in your success or failure? Are they afraid to hurt your feelings? Have you really listened? Have you prepared for every possible outcome? Have you gone through every angle that makes sense? Have you addressed every question, issue, and insecurity to your best ability? Are you holding on to something that needs to be eliminated or adjusted? Do you know and understand your competitive set? What makes your product different than anyone else's? Can it be easily copied? Do you know how to price it? Do you know how to market it? Do you know how to distribute it? If you don't have answers, do you know who to ask?

Sharing Space: Allow yourself to stretch physically, mentally and spiritually so that you and your new idea can coexist.

Key Questions.

What kind of support do you have? Do you know what you are willing to sacrifice? Are you carrying any old habits that will compromise your success or your happiness? Are you fully engaged? Have you consciously and deliberately managed the balance with all areas of your life? Have you done all your homework? Do you know your target audience? Have you talked to them? Have you answered every question? Have you thanked the people who have helped you?

Contractions: Just before delivery, chaos will surface. It will be painful. Learn to trust and breathe.

<u>Key Questions.</u>

Have you been clear and deliberate in your leadership of this project? Are you aware of the effect that you have had on others? Has everyone seen your vision in detail? Do they fully understand it? Have you communicated the brand personality? Do you have the resources to do what you need to do? Are they reliable? Are they trustworthy? Are you prepared for the chaos? Are you ready for major things to go wrong? Where is your support? Will they be there when you need them?

Delivery: Strength is required for the final transition.

<u>Key Questions.</u>

Is your new creation everything you thought it would be? Upon reflection, is there anything you would have done differently? Is there an underlying model for you to follow? Did other ideas surface that you are ready to conceive?

Congratulations and Happy Birthing!

ABOUT THE AUTHOR

April Jeffries has led innovation teams at major marketing companies such as Campbell Soup and Pinnacle Foods. She has a Bachelor of Science degree in Mechanical Engineering from the Massachusetts Institute of Technology, was awarded an MBA in Marketing from the Wharton School of Business and holds a Certificate in Multimedia Technology from New York University. In addition, April is a professionally trained actress and award winning writer / producer of original works in various mediums. Connect with her online at www.ideabirthing.com.

"Show me your ways, O Lord, teach me your paths"

Psalm 25:4

Made in the USA
Charleston, SC
02 November 2012